Tough Times

by Clare Beswick and Sally Featherstone

Published 2009 by A&C Black Publishers Limited
36 Soho Square, London W1D 3QY
www.acblack.com

ISBN 978-1408-114-64-3

Text © Clare Beswick and Sally Featherstone
Design © Sally Boothroyd 2009
Illustrations © Kerry Ingham and Martha Hardy

A CIP record for this publication is available from the British Library.

Printed in Great Britain by Latimer Trend & Company Limited

This book is produced using paper that is made from wood grown in
managed, sustainable forests. It is natural, renewable and recyclable.
The logging and manufacturing processes conform to the environmental
regulations of the country of origin.

To see our full range of titles
visit **www.acblack.com**

Contents

Introduction

From time to time, we all encounter difficult times, when circumstances present new challenges and demands. **Tough Times** is for early years practitioners working with babies and young children under five who are struggling to cope with new circumstances and difficult emotions. **Tough Times** builds on the principles, themes and good practice described in the EYFS framework and provides practitioners and parents with practical ideas and tips to help very young children cope with those tricky times in their lives.

The activities in this series are designed specially for use in one-to-one or very small group situations to meet the additional needs of individual children at a time of stress. They also:

- use everyday objects and toys readily available in your setting or home

- are quick and easy to do

- encourage children to express their feelings

- have plenty of extra ideas for taking activities further if needed

- take account of the needs of babies and very young children.

I want my mum!

This topic looks at separation anxiety: when a child becomes distressed when their parent or carer tries to leave them with someone else. Advice on how to reassure both the child and the parent is given as well as a variety of different activities to help the child cope with the separation and settle into the early years setting.

It's mine!

This topic is about possession, turn-taking and sharing. As well as ideas on sharing resources in the setting, there are activities that focus on sharing time and attention and understanding the needs of others.

Losing it!

This topic examines anger: possible causes, strategies to calm a child who is having a tantrum and activities where children can express their angry emotions in a safe, controlled way.

I can't do it!

This topic explores children's self-esteem and confidence. Reasons for why a child may have low self-esteem are suggested, and methods on how to tackle these issues are outlined alongside confidence-boosting activities to develop a 'can-do' attitude.

Who's this?

This topic looks at ways that a child may feel and react when a new baby is born into their family and they are no longer the centre of attention. Activities are suggested to help them adjust to their new role in the family and regain their sense of security.

Where am I going?

This topic is for when a child's family is moving house or the child is experiencing another major change in their family life that is causing them distress. It provides activities to help them deal with and adapt to new and unfamiliar circumstances.

Tough Times: The EYFS

The EYFS and Tough Times

The Early Years Foundation Stage (EYFS), DfES 2007 is the comprehensive framework which sets the standards for learning, development and care of children from birth to five years. Central to the framework are key themes and principles, including that every child is unique and

> '... is a competent learner from birth who can be resilient, capable, confident and self assured.'

The EYFS framework identifies six areas of learning and development. These are:

- Personal, Social and Emotional Development
- Communication, Language and Literacy
- Problem Solving, Reasoning and Numeracy
- Knowledge and Understanding of the World
- Physical Development
- Creative Development

The topics in Tough Times focus on aspects within the area of Personal Social and Emotional Development. They will help you to develop and support children's self-esteem and self confidence.

They also support the development of young children's emotional literacy, enabling them to understand and express their feelings, and cope with new challenges and difficult situations in life.

I Want My Mum!
Easing separation anxiety

Contents

Introduction

Separation anxiety is a perfectly ordinary and expected phase in babies' and young children's development. How each baby or young child is affected by this anxiety varies hugely and is influenced by many factors, including:

- personality

- developmental stage

- earlier experiences

- position in the family and the attention they are used to in relationships with key people in their life

- self-esteem, confidence and the ability to trust others

- the confidence of key people in their lives

- the environment

- the response of those they are being left with

- time of day

- hunger, tiredness or over stimulation

- many other factors unique to each child and each separation.

A parent leaving when they are wanted is going to leave a very young child feeling horrified that they are not all powerful in their world! The discovery that the world does not revolve around them is a painful discovery for some children. This is not to say they have been spoilt or over indulged, just that they are at a stage developmentally where they are egocentric with little understanding of the needs of others.

What you might see and what the child might be feeling

Every child and every environment and set of circumstances in which a child is experiencing separation anxiety is different, but very young children will show us what they are feeling. They may have very strong feelings that they don't understand and almost certainly won't be able to express with words, so it is important to 'look, listen and note', that is, carefully observe, consider and interpret what you see as the child expresses their feelings and needs.

A child may express their anxiety in many different ways, including:

- clinging to an adult
- angry or silent tears
- shouting, screaming and temper tantrums
- hurting themselves, for example, biting their hand
- becoming very withdrawn
- refusing to eat or refusing to join in
- wetting or soiling.

Any unexpected difference or change in behaviour should be noted and the cause considered. A child might be feeling any or all of these:

sad

angry   confused

lost   fearful   panicked

rejected   out of control

jealous

Hellos and goodbyes
A simple routine to begin and end each session

What you need

- A small teddy bear

- A small hanky-size piece of soft fabric

What you do

1. As soon as the child arrives, stand with the parent. Get down to the child's level so you can gaze easily into each other's eyes. Give the child the teddy bear to hold.

2. Smile and sing to the child. Using a simple bright voice, sing:
   It's a new day, it's a new day and I say,
   Hello, hello to you.
   It's a new day, it's a new day and I say
   Hello, hello to Ted.
   Welcome to our day
   What shall we do? Let's go and play.

3. Move gently into the nursery and stand with the child and watch the activities. When the parent is ready to go, say clearly to the child, 'Time for mummy to go. See you later mummy'. Pause for the parent to give the child a very brief kiss and then, as the parent moves towards the door, ask the child, 'Can teddy wave goodbye?'.

4. Give the child the small piece of fabric to wave goodbye. Make sure the parent knows that, having said goodbye, they need to make a calm but firm exit.

5. If the child is distressed, a second member of staff needs to reassure the parent once they are out of the child's sight.

Being there – playing, watching, listening, talking

- Make this activity a priority every session. Routine is the key.

- Speak and move slowly with the child, avoiding the busiest and noisiest parts of the setting. An anxious child needs gentle reassurance and acknowledgement of the way they are feeling, not distraction.

- Comment carefully on what the other children are doing, drawing the child's attention to the possibilities of getting involved in the play.

- Allow time for the child to calm themselves and give them specific praise for becoming calm, such as, 'I think saying goodbye to mummy this morning was really hard, but you are safe and have done really well to come in and see what we have to play with today'.

- Give the anxious child regular reassuring smiles and thumbs up throughout the session.

More ideas

- Agree with other practitioners in the setting a simple goodbye song to be sung with all the children at the end of each session.

- Create a poster for the parents' noticeboard about what the setting does to help children to settle into each session.

- Ask the children to select a smiley, okay or sad face to show their key person how they are feeling when they first arrive in the session.

Specially for babies

- Involve parents in deciding a goodbye routine before the session in which they plan to leave their baby for the first time.

- Keep goodbyes to parents calm and unrushed, but planned and brief.

- Make sure parents feel confident that they are able to bring their baby's comfort object to the setting, and that it will be respected and well cared for and, most importantly, returned safely at the end of the session.

What next?

Making sense of the day

What you need

- A digital camera
- Index cards
- A shoe box
- Scissors
- Sticky tape

What you do

1. Take photos of the key parts of the session, such as the children playing indoors, playing outside, snack/mealtimes, story time and so on.

2. Print these photos and mount them onto index cards.

3. Cut a slot in the lid of the shoe box to make a simple posting box.

4. With the child, choose up to four photos that will show them the order of their day, and fix these to the wall.

5. Talk to the child simply about the order of the day, including the point at which they will be reunited with their parent/carer.

6. As each part of the day depicted by a photograph passes, help the child to find the right photo and post it into the box.

7. Post the last card with the parent and child together.

Being there – playing, watching, listening, talking

- Keep your language simple, and speak slowly and gently to the child.

- When you see the child happy and relaxed, comment positively, such as, 'you look like you are having fun', so that the child can recognise positive moments in the session.

- Spend time watching with the child. Allow plenty of time for them to observe the other children and make their own decisions as to when they are ready to get involved.

- At group time, allow the child to sit next to quietly confident children who will be sensitive to their anxiety.

More ideas

- Create the activity timetable on an interactive whiteboard.

- Fix Velcro dots to the back of the photos so the child can create their own photo timetable as they gain more confidence.

- Use photos to offer choices of activities to the child.

- Add a photo to the timetable of the parent and child together at the beginning and end of the session.

Specially for babies

- For older babies and very young children, substitute the photos for everyday objects, such as a cup for snack time, a hat for outdoor play, a book for story time and so on.

- Give the youngest babies consistent situational clues to help to develop their understanding of the session's routines, such as putting a hat in their hands and saying 'time to go outside' before getting them ready to go outside, or perhaps giving them an empty cup and saying 'dinner time', before lifting them into a chair for their dinner, and so on.

- Remember, separation anxiety is a perfectly ordinary part of child development. Reassure parents of this with a calm, assured approach.

It's special to me

Comfort toys from home

What you need

- A wicker basket
- Small pieces of thin card
- Felt pens
- Ribbon
- A single hole punch

What you do

1. Ask a key person to talk to parents about the value of comfort toys and invite them to bring their child's comforter to the setting. Explain carefully what provision will be made to make sure that it is only accessible to their child.

2. Reassure the child and parents that great care will be taken to avoid comforter objects being misplaced.

3. Help the child to make a special name tag for their comfort toy using the felt pens and card. Punch a hole in the tag, thread a length of ribbon through it and use it to label the comforter.

4. Place the comfort toy in the wicker basket. Explain to all the children in the setting that this is name's special toy and that it is to stay in the basket.

5. Let the child have the toy each time they need it, but also regularly invite them to return the toy to the basket.

6. When they are busy with an activity, ask if you might put the toy in the basket for a few minutes.

7. As the child grows in confidence and asks for the toy, encourage them to bring the basket closer, but leave the toy in the basket to touch, but not hold.

Being there – playing, watching, listening, talking

- Observe the child carefully and identify what triggers their need for the comfort toy.

- Talk about how the child feels when they have their comfort toy.

- Model the language the child needs to express their feelings.

- Listen to the child's developing use of language to express their needs and feelings.

More ideas

- Try a small group Circle time activity focused on comfort objects.
- Bring in your old comfort object/old soft toy to show the child.
- Read *Dogger* by Shirley Hughes (Red Fox).
- Read *Alfie Gets in First* by Shirley Hughes (Red Fox). Share the story of Alfie getting locked in the house alone, and talk about the way Alfie feels and other experiences that can make us feel sad, scared or alone.

Specially for babies

- Make time to sit quietly with the baby. Provide them with their comfort object, enjoy some quiet finger play together, give a little hand massage whilst listening to relaxing music.

- Try to think ahead and make the comforter available before the baby becomes distressed, perhaps as you see them becoming tired, or maybe during busier or noisier times in the setting.

- Make sure all staff know where the child's comforter is kept and that it is to be returned to the parent/carer at the end of each session.

How much longer?

Using timers with older children

What you need

- A selection of different timers, such as a sand timer, kitchen timer or a simple alarm clock, and a card clock template for matching

What you do

1. When calm, show the older child the cardboard clock set to the current time. Talk about the hands of the clock and the numbers they are pointing to.

2. Look at, and talk about, how this matches the clock in the setting.

3. Tell the child what time the parent or carer will be returning to the setting, and show them this on the cardboard clock. Ask them where they would like to leave the cardboard clock and agree to check back to the clock regularly to see how time is progressing towards pick-up time.

4. Use the sand timers or kitchen timer to measure together how long some everyday activities or routines take, such as how long they played outside, how long story time is and so on.

5. Model language that helps the child to develop an understanding of time, such as 'next', 'before', 'after', 'soon', 'later' and so on.

6. At home time, show the child how the cardboard clock matches the clock in the setting.

Being there – playing, watching, listening, talking

- Listen to the language the child uses to report what has happened previously and also to predict ahead.

- Watch to see which activities absorb the child and which activities or situations are most likely to cause the child anxiety.

- Think about the changeover times in the nursery, such as end of group times, a tidy-up time and so on, and consider how best to support the child who is taking a while to settle in the setting.

- Consider the child's understanding of time and what clues they rely on to follow the progression of the session towards the time when their parent/carer will arrive.

More ideas

- Talk to parents about possible triggers for unexpected separation anxiety, such as changes to the child's routine at home or the arrival of a new baby.

- All children will enjoy *I Love My Mummy* by Sebastien Braun (Boxer Books), a beautiful picture book showing a young animal, discovering the world supported by its mother – a great opener for conversations about feelings. There is a companion book titled *I Love My Daddy*.

- For children who may have a parent who is away for a long period of time, look at *Daddy, Will You Miss Me?* by Wendy McCormick (Aladdin Books).

- For children whose parents work long hours, try *When Mummy Comes Home Tonight* by Eileen Spinelli (Simon & Schuster Children's Books).

Specially for babies

- Use consistent simple language to reassure babies who are anxious on separation and be kind but honest about when their parent will return.

- Try dancing and gently rocking a distressed baby.

- Use distraction sensitively. It is important to acknowledge the baby's distress before attempting to distract them.

- Bubbles and a gentle blowing on the baby's hands often capture even the most anxious baby's attention.

A safe place to watch

Building a den or an oasis

What you need

- A net curtain or similar
- A cushion
- Pegs
- A soft toy of the child's choice

What you do

1. Talk to the parent about the importance of all children watching and gaining confidence before joining in with activities and play.

2. Help the child to build a simple den by pegging the net curtain up in a suitable corner so they can create a safe hidey hole where they can watch the other children from a quieter spot.

3. Make the corner comfortable for the child with the cushion and the soft toy.

4. Share a book together in the den and then spend a little time quietly watching the other children.

5. Comment on what the children are doing.

6. Allow the child to use this den or oasis whenever they wish. Keep it a quiet spot for watching.

Being there – playing, watching, listening, talking

- Observe the child's use of the den. Are there particular triggers before they decide to spend some time watching from the den? What do they find comforting about the den? What entices them out of it?

- Listen to the child's comments as they talk about the setting. Observe their body language and consider how to help them move towards exploring the setting more fully.

- Talk to the child, commenting on what they can see from the oasis. Try to avoid direct questions but give the child plenty of opportunities to make non-verbal responses.

- Remember to offer and respect the child's choices.

More ideas

- Remember some children will need a quiet space or corner to observe outdoor play.

- Big cardboard boxes can be used to create great dens with the addition of just a blanket.

- Try to use semi-transparent fabric in the oasis to allow the child to feel hidden and unobserved, but giving them a clear view of the other children's play.

- A simple finger-friendly rocking horse or similar rocking chair/toy is a very comforting place to sit and watch.

Specially for babies

- Personalise the child's seat or play space.

- Try to keep meal times, personal care and play routines as consistent as possible.

- Start and end each session with a consistent routine. Try using the same picture book or song to begin and end each day.

- Create a treasure basket of familiar objects personal to the baby and their family, such as one of their socks, a parent's glove, one of their soft toys and so on.

Where's my mum/dad?

Using a simple storyboard

What you need

- About six index cards
- Pens
- Blu-tack

What you do

1. Talk to the child about their day. On each card, draw together a simple fun line drawing to illustrate part of the day – the first part may be getting ready for school: getting dressed, brushing teeth and coming to the setting.

2. On the second card, draw saying goodbye to their parent, then playing. Ask the child to talk about and draw key parts of the session. Together, create about six story cards illustrating the child's day up to being collected from the session and where they go next, maybe home on the bus or to another Early Years setting.

3. Fix these to a low door or wall. Talk to the child often during the session, looking together at the storyboard and finding out where the child is in the story. Talk about things that make them feel happy, sad, nervous, excited and so on at each stage of their day.

Being there – playing, watching, listening, talking

- Observe the child's body language carefully – it often tells you more about how they are feeling than their words.

- Try to model the language they need to use to express their feelings.

- Allow plenty of time for watching.

- Offer the distressed child quiet, unfussy reassurance. Often, a simple gentle touch of the child's hands or a gentle blow on their face is enough to comfort and reassure them.

More ideas

- Create a parallel set of cards for a parent's day, describing what they did before the session, what they are doing while the child is with you and finishing with them collecting the child. Be sure to make their day sound boring!

- Create a storyboard using felt figures and shapes on a felt board.

- Draw outline pictures on an overhead transparency and project this on to a blank wall or cupboard.

- Use play people and Lego to talk about and play through the child's and parents' day.

- Share books about the first day at nursery, for suggested books see the resources section on pages 103–110.

Specially for babies

- Use real everyday objects and a doll or teddy bear to model simple pretend play.

- Encourage older babies to wave goodbye and blow a kiss as a clear signal that their parent is leaving.

- Make sure all parents say goodbye to their baby before leaving, rather than trying to leave while the baby is distracted. Explain to parents the importance of being honest, calm and confident about leaving, as well as the importance of trust to even the youngest baby.

My special note

A useful prop for older children

What you need

- Heart, flower and star shaped note paper
- Pens
- Star or smiley face stickers

What you do

1. Invite the parent to sit with their child for a few moments to create a special 'love you' note for the child.

2. Encourage the child to be involved, making marks, choosing stickers and so on.

3. Ask the parent to offer the child choices of where they want to keep their special note, such as tucked in a pocket, in a little bag or so on.

4. Ask older children to make a special note for their parent to keep with them.

5. Tell the child that anytime they are wondering what their parent is doing, or are feeling a little sad or afraid, they can look at their very special note.

Being there – playing, watching, listening, talking

- Make sure the child is very much a part of the note making and choices.

- Talk to the child about special mementoes that you have, such as special jewellery or photos that help you to remember special people.

- Look together at the note the parent and child have created from time to time in the session. Acknowledge its importance to the child and their feelings of longing.

- Regular show and tell sessions allow all children to make a clear link between home and the setting. Less confident children can bring in objects for you to show and tell on their behalf.

More ideas

- Encourage the parent and child to make a simple message bracelet – a strip of thin card decorated with stickers and a special message from the parent to the child. Fix this loosely around the child's wrist by taping the ends together.

- Simple twisted or plaited friendship bracelets are fun and special for parents and older children to make together.

- For Charlie and Lola fans, share the story of Lola's invisible friend who was too nervous to start school, *I Am Too Absolutely Small for School* by Lauren Child (Orchard Books) and then visit www.charlieandlola.com for simple games and lots of fun printables.

Specially for babies

- Discuss with the parent the sort of things that help the baby to settle.

- There are many models of communication passports that can be adapted for babies and very young children in your setting. See the resources section for useful websites. Passports are a great way of ensuring that everyone in the setting is aware of the baby's needs, likes and dislikes, as well as being an excellent focus for discussion between a parent and key person.

Magic Ted

Teddy bear/hand-puppet play

What you need

- A teddy or simple hand puppet
- A hairbrush and flannel
- A cup
- A tissue
- A small picture book
- A toy car
- A tiny scarf/ribbon

What you do

1. Play with the child, modelling simple pretend play. Help the child to 'wash' and brush teddy. Talk about the sort of things the child does at home with their family before they come to the setting.

2. Give teddy a drink and try to use words to describe how teddy might be feeling, such as tired, hungry, thirsty and so on. Also model language to describe emotions, such as happy, sad, excited, scared and so on.

3. Using simple pretend play, take teddy through the main parts of the nursery day, starting with saying goodbye to parents and then moving onto other activities, such as playing, getting wrapped up to play outside, having a snack and story time.

4. Ask open questions to encourage the child to think about how teddy might be feeling.

Being there – playing, watching, listening, talking

- Play alongside the child, modelling simple pretend play and providing a simple commentary to describe actions.

- Watch to see how the child imitates actions and listen to the language they use to describe how teddy might be feeling.

- Observe how they relate to teddy or another hand puppet. Do they become absorbed in the activity?

More ideas

- Ask the child to suggest other activities for teddy. Talk about which activities she/he likes and why.

- Talk together about any parts of the session that teddy doesn't enjoy and see if together you can consider strategies to make these parts of the day easier for him/her.

- Encourage the child to keep teddy with them for the session. From time to time, ask them how teddy is feeling and give the puppet a smiley sticker each time she/he is happy and relaxed. If the child tells you teddy is sad, acknowledge his/her feelings and talk about how teddy can be made to feel better.

Specially for babies

- Introduce simple turn-taking imitation play with young babies, such as patting a drum in turn, splashing water in turn, or taking turns with making sounds. Begin the turn-taking sequence by copying an action the baby is making.

- Look out for simple photo board books of babies' and peoples' faces, such as *Baby Faces* by Sandra Lousada (Campbell Books). Use simple, short two- and three-word phrases to label the pictures. Introduce action and describing words to older babies.

- Older babies and very young children will enjoy *Captain Pike Looks After the Baby* by Marjorie Newman (Macmillan). It provides a great opportunity to introduce new words to describe our emotions.

A 'Well done' rosette

Celebrating small steps

What you need

- A length of broad ribbon
- A small circle of thick card
- Strong glue
- Sticky tape

What you do

1. Fix the end of the ribbon to the edge of the circle of card. Slowly pleat the ribbon around the edge of the card. Ask the child to place plenty of clear glue on the edge of the card and to fix the pleats. Work together, chatting about rosettes and trophies as you go.

2. Finish the rosette by asking the child to draw a smiley face or star in the centre of the rosette.

3. When the glue has dried, fix the rosette to the child's clothing using a simple circle of sticky tape fixed to the back of the rosette. Talk to the child about why you feel they have earned this rosette, maybe for calming themselves down when their parent left, waving goodbye bravely, getting busy with the activities, watching and being with the other children, or maybe holding something for you while you worked with the other children.

Being there – playing, watching, listening, talking

- Offer the child simple choices, for example, ask 'should we use the red or blue ribbon?' and so on. Try to involve them as much as possible in the making of the rosette.

- Talk together about the way we mark celebrations and achievements, such as birthday cakes, sporting medals, clapping hands and so on.

- Talk about the different ways of saying goodbye to people: waving, hugging, kissing, watching as they go, saying goodbye at an activity area, saying goodbye at the door and so on. Talk about how you greet and say goodbye to other people. Listen to the child talking about their experiences at home and in the setting. Try to make links between what they say about home and what happens in the setting.

More ideas

- Use skin-friendly face paints to draw smiley faces or stars on a child's hand to remind them to say goodbye to parents bravely, or for describing their feelings to you.

- Reward children with simple stickers for calming down if distressed. Offer choices of sticker pictures.

- Create a range of certificate templates for rewards at the end of a session. For lots of ideas and free printable resources, visit www.sparklebox.co.uk.

- Cut simple trophy and medal shapes from card and either paint or spray-paint in silver or gold, or cover in shiny foil paper.

Specially for babies

- Keep a special splash pat mat or similar activity to use as a reward when older babies have calmed after separation.

- Create a special treasure basket of intriguing items for the older baby to explore as soon as they are settled. For a plethora of treasure basket ideas, see *The Little Book of Treasure Baskets* (Featherstone).

- For a soothing time, choose a warm soft-textured blanket and allow the child to explore this texture, and the texture of other furry objects.

- Be sure to exclude other possible reasons why the baby might be distressed aside from separation, such as teething, hunger, tiredness, sudden noises and so on.

It's in the book

Story time ideas to say goodbye

What you need

- *Goodnight Miffy* by Dick Bruna (Methuen Books).

- A toy clock, socks, shoes, small train and a small ball

- A large plastic box

- A small blanket or similar

What you do

1. Share this simple board book with the child, encouraging them to imitate waving goodbye to each object as you turn over each page.

2. Explore the objects and play at matching them to the pictures in the book.

3. Next, retell the story using the objects, waving goodbye to each object as the child puts it into the box.

4. At the end of the story, cover the box with the blanket. Pause and then, using a surprised voice, say 'Where's the ball?' and so on, helping the child to find each item in turn under the blanket.

Being there – playing, watching, listening, talking

- Chat with the children about bedtime routines with an emphasis on feeling words, such as warm, sleepy, calm and so on.

- Think about each child's attention skills. Ask yourself about the importance of the props?

- Listen to the language used, identifying spontaneous and imitated phrases and for the child linking the story and props to their own experiences.

More ideas

- Play lots of simple hide and seek and peek-a-boo type games to encourage babies' and children's understanding of object permanence.

- Check out the the resources section on pages 103–110 for excellent books which deal with saying goodbye and parting.

- Use puppets and simple everyday objects as props and invite maybe one or two other children to enjoy sharing these stories. Encourage them to talk about their own feelings and experiences.

Specially for babies

- Invite the parent to give the child a 'special kiss on the palm of the baby's hand' to keep for the session.

- Make goodbyes calm, planned, kind and *short*. Gone is gone. In order for the child to understand the parent has gone but is coming back, reassure quietly but don't prolong – a swift goodbye is best.

How do I feel right now?

Expressing and recording feelings

What you need

- Felt pens
- Sticky labels and small pieces of card
- A simple posting box

What you do

1. Together, use the pens to create a different smiley face emoticon on each of the labels. Create happy faces, tired faces, sad faces, a sad face with a teddy (to mean 'I need my special toy/comforter') and one label with lots of happy faces (to mean 'happy with my friends').

2. Talk with the child as you make the labels together, focusing on words to describe feelings. Try to show empathy and also help the child to realise that you and other children also have similar feelings at different times.

3. Stick the labels onto the cards.

4. Spread the cards out and encourage the child and, in time, maybe one or two more children, to choose the card/label that best describes how they feel and to post it into the box.

5. Be sure to reassure and comfort the child, acknowledging their feelings and providing support, comfort and distraction as appropriate to meet the needs expressed.

Being there – playing, watching, listening, talking

- Consider the range of words you use and encourage the child to use them to describe feelings and emotions.

- Watch to see how the child is expressing themselves using body language.

- Think about what prompts you can best use to engage children with this activity.

- Observe schemas that the child may be using and try to adapt the activity to best suit the child's individual needs.

More ideas

- Revisit this activity at key times in the session, particularly at the beginning and the end.

- Extend this activity to circle time with a small group of children.

- Leave a few cards blank so the children can create their own emoticons.

- Use Google to find free smiley face emoticons . You will find lots of animated and printable smiley faces showing a wide range of characters and emoticons – fun to look at together with lots of opportunities for talking about feelings and facial expressions.

Specially for babies

- Find photos of real babies expressing a wide range of feelings and emotions, and display these in simple picture pockets.

- Model simple pretend play, such as 'dolly crying', 'dolly sad' or 'teddy jumping', 'teddy happy' and so on.

- Read *The Social Baby* by Lynne Murray and Liz Andrews (The Children's Project) for in-depth advice on observing babies and tuning into babies' needs.

What did I do today?

Building links with home

What you need

- A talking photo album! Originally designed for the blind but now widely available, these simple books allow you to add your own pictures and photographs, and you can record a sound bite for each. The photos can be changed easily and messages re-recorded, bespoke to each child's needs.

- Star stickers

- A digital camera and mini printer

What you do

1. Take photos of key activities and times during the child's day or week and print them together.

2. Choose photos to include in the album to best reflect the child's week. Check out what they felt was the highlight of the week.

3. Together, record a sound bite or mini message about the activity. Again, focus on words to describe feelings.

4. Put the photos and recorded messages together in the album. Talk about how the child felt during each activity, if it helped them feel at home in the setting and so on. Help the child to add stars to favourite activity images.

Being there – playing, watching, listening, talking

- Observe the child's responses as they share the book with other children, adults and family. Help the child to use appropriate words to describe their feelings.

- Encourage the child to join in the recording process, verbally or non-verbally by pressing buttons and so on.

- As you look at the album together offer specific praise for completing activities, joining in games, taking turns and so on.

- Help the child to think about and talk about how other children in the pictures might be feeling.

- Identify the activities that the child went to after they had said goodbye to their parent/carer and also comment on the last activity of the session before being reunited with their carer.

More ideas

- Tear or cut pictures from resource catalogues and magazines showing favourite toys and activities.

- Use Talking Tins and Talking Badges as a great way to give instant reward to a child for settling into an activity. See www.talkingproducts.co.uk and www.inclusive.co.uk for more ideas and inspiration.

- Ask parents to help the child to bring in a memento of an activity they have done together, maybe a bus ticket or ice cream wrapper and so on. Talk about these with the child, focusing on how they felt and who they were with.

- Play alongside the child with play people in small world play. Encourage scenarios that involve people arriving, travelling and saying goodbye, maybe a train station or children getting on a bus to go to school. Provide a simple commentary using short phrases at a level appropriate to the child's understanding.

Specially for babies

- Encourage parents to borrow a toy from your setting, to play with their baby at home, and then return it.

- Look out for board books with lots of babies' faces and different facial expressions. Encourage parents to share these with their babies.

- Develop a simple tickle or giggle game with the baby and then encourage the parent to play this simple game in the same way at home too.

Advice

Try to create a calm, ordered and warm atmosphere within the setting. Provide a wealth of opportunities for all children, from the quieter, less-confident children to the wildly enthusiastic, confident children. Be a good role model, listening carefully and responding appropriately, tuning into the needs of the children and the parents. Be confident and trust your instincts – a calm, happy, focused practitioner is just the sort of key person an anxious child needs.

Tips for practitioners when faced with a distraught child:

- Use a calm, quiet voice.

- Offer gentle physical reassurance.

- Give the child a soft toy to hold/hug.

- Use simple words of comfort.

- Acknowledge the strength of the child's feelings.

- Provide reassurance that the parent will be back after … (be specific – not just back later).

- Sit at the child's level, alongside them.

- Provide opportunities for the child to be distracted but don't force it.

- Offer a warm, welcoming space for the child to watch.

- Be consistent.

- Ensure parents make a swift and calm goodbye/exit.

- Ask a colleague to provide support to the parent, out of sight and hearing of their distressed child.

- Praise the child as they calm down and gain control of the way they are expressing their feelings.

- Create a gentle, kind, warm but light atmosphere – you are sorry the child is upset, but everything is okay and the play session can continue uninterrupted.

- Don't make a big fuss.

Reassure parents by:

- explaining this is a perfectly ordinary part of child development

- planning together how you can help the child to overcome these feelings of anxiety

- avoiding blame – some children are naturally more anxious than others

- talking about what you do in the setting to help all children understand the day

- agreeing how you will let the parents know their child has settled

- planning to review how it's going every few days

- sharing some of the activities in this book – that way, parents will feel they are making a real contribution towards helping their child to settle.

It's Mine!

Learning to share

Contents

Introduction

Learning about possession, turn taking and sharing are all important parts of the Early Years Foundation Stage. They are crucial elements to all six areas of learning but are key to personal, social and emotional development, and to all aspects of communication.

Being able to share time, attention and resources are all important features of positive relationships and are fundamental to children's happiness and ability to be a successful part of a group.

Developing the skill of sharing attention and the joy of sharing and celebrating others' successes are very important attributes.

To develop these skills and understanding, babies and very young children need to:

- have self-confidence
- be self-reliant
- have some awareness of the needs of others
- have experienced effective role models
- have enjoyed constructive, rewarding relationships with adults and other children
- be given opportunities to explore resources uninterrupted on their own as well as part of a small group
- have reached developmental stages in communication and thinking skills that enable them to understand others
- respond to routine, consistency and clarity.

Early Years practitioners should know that every day, children within their setting are slowly moving towards an understanding of the needs of others, as well as sharing, turn taking, and enjoying shared attention with other children and significant adults.

Much of this is down to practitioners and parents providing enabling environments, consistency, and by developing rewarding and positive relationships within the setting. Most importantly, this development is part of the progress that children make across the Early Years Foundation Stage.

What you might see and what the child might be feeling

Most children will make steady progress in this area as a natural part of the range of experiences and opportunities they encounter pre-school. However, a few children will, from time to time, experience very real difficulties, causing themselves and others in the setting considerable distress and frustration. This can encourage an inability to share, which can become a significant barrier to learning and friendships.

Practitioners may observe children:

- snatching
- biting
- screaming
- pleading
- hiding
- sulking
- making silent protest.

Children may be feeling:

confused   anxious

angry   frustrated   uncertain

frightened   alone

Mine, yours, his, hers

Understanding possession

What you need

- A basket

- A collection of everyday personal possessions belonging to the child and you, including, for example, shoes, socks, hat, book, jumper, bag, gloves, cup, spoon and so on

What you do

1. Place all the everyday personal possessions in the basket.

2. Spin the basket round, counting 'one, two, three' together, then stop.

3. Take turns to remove one item, and then say 'mine' or 'yours' as appropriate.

4. Give the child plenty of time to examine the objects and try them on as appropriate. Talk about the function of each object as well as possession, such as:

   Adult gloves: 'to keep my hands warm', 'mine' and so on.

   Try to convey a sense of care when handling the objects, encouraging the child to handle the possessions with respect.

Being there – playing, watching, listening, talking

- Check if the child recognises their possessions and understands the concept of 'yours' and 'mine'.

- Listen to the way they use the language of possession spontaneously, such as 'my hat', 'your shoes' or '*name's* bag'.

- Watch to see if the child is able to demonstrate the function of objects, such as pretending to drink from the cup and so on.

More ideas

- Sort photos and pictures of objects into 'yours' and 'mine'.

- Sort according to colour, giving all the red buttons to the picture of a girl and all the green ones to the picture of a boy. Ask 'Is it his or hers?'.

- Play alongside the child, bathing boy and girl dolls. Comment as the child plays, such as 'washing her face', 'shampooing his hair' and so on.

- Play dressing paper dolls. Emphasise key possession words, such as 'yours', 'mine' and so on.

Specially for babies

- Play simple singing games, tickling different body parts on the baby to emphasise body part words, such as 'tickle on the nose'.

- Try some simple pretend play together: brush dolly's hair, wash dolly's face and so on.

- Create a treasure basket of personal possessions that belong to the baby and to one of the baby's parents. Identify the items: daddy's sock, mummy's hat, *name's* vest and so on.

One for you, one for me
Sharing

What you need

- A simple stamp set (one stamp and one ink pad)
- Ticket-sized cards in two colours
- Scrap paper

What you do

1. Help the child to sort the tickets according to colour: one colour for the child and one for you.
2. Practise using the ink pad and stamp on the scrap paper.
3. Ask the child to stamp one of your tickets.
4. Invite them to choose one of their own tickets for you to stamp.
5. Continue to practise sorting, sharing and turn taking.
6. Praise each stamp made and, most importantly, each time the stamp is offered to you for your turn.
7. Prompt with an outstretched hand and a thank you.

Being there – playing, watching, listening, talking

- Observe in which activities the child is most able to share resources.
- Watch the child's body language prior to them snatching or grabbing a resource from another child.
- Consider what motivates the child. What rewards are most effective?
- Use key words, such as 'yours', 'mine', 'ours', 'next', 'share' and so on.
- Think about what the child understands about sharing. Are they able to maintain a sense of shared attention and pleasure in another child's successes?

More ideas

- Invite the child to offer around small snacks.
- Encourage the child to hold a special teddy at story time and then to invite another child not to hold the toy but give the teddy a blanket/hat and so on.
- Find activities that take two, such as a simple rocker, push-you-pull me toys, playing with long hoses and a water jug and so on.

Specially for babies

- Encourage babies to play alongside each other, maybe sharing one pat mat, reaching for the same baby gym mobiles, standing together to pop bubbles in front of a wall-mounted mirror and so on.
- With another practitioner and another baby, each hold your baby facing away from you and towards the other baby. Dance and sing gently together.
- Encourage babies to push trundle trucks together.
- Provide a huge bowl of cooked spaghetti and encourage two babies to explore together using just their fingers.

My go NOW!

Taking turns

What you need

- A long tube, fixed or flexible (a long cardboard tube or perhaps a long flexible tumble drier ventilation hose or similar)
- Small balls

What you do

1. Peek through the tube at each other.
2. Reach into the tube.
3. Take turns to explore the tube.
4. Hold the tube at the child's height at a slope so that they can roll a ball down the tube.
5. Now it is your turn. Ask the child to hold the tube so you can have your turn. Be clear that it is one ball each. If necessary, place all the balls in a small bag or box that you control!

Being there – playing, watching, listening, talking

- Try to anticipate the child's rising frustration at having to take turns and distract them by changing the direction or angle of the slope.
- Use your voice to make this activity exciting and varied.
- Observe how long the child can maintain the game.
- Use very simple, short repetitive phrases to focus the child on turn taking.

More ideas

- Invite another child to join you and encourage the two children to take turns.
- Roll the balls down the tube into a paddling pool or puddle outside.
- Try posting other toys down the tube, such as small cars, sound makers and so on.
- Take turns with marble runs or the traditional toy, 'clown on a ladder'.
- Use really runny paint and encourage the child to drizzle the paint over a large sheet of paper on an easel. Encourage them to take turns with you or another child at the easel, working together on the same paper but with just one brush to share.

Specially for babies

- Begin by imitating the baby as they pat an object. When they have noticed that you are copying their action or rhythm, continue for a few turns, then change the action very slightly to focus the baby on the turn-taking element of the game.
- Look out for toys with instant reward, such as knocking down towers of bricks, jack in the box, wind-up toys and so on.
- For anticipation before turn taking, play 'ready, steady, go' games.

Ticket time
Sharing and active play

What you need

- Lots of wheeled toys
- Chalk
- Masking tape
- Thin card
- A motoring magazine
- Scissors and glue
- A small bag or box to hold the card pieces
- A kitchen timer or similar audible timer

What you do

1. Use the chalk and masking tape to create a simple road or track circuit on the floor outside.

2. Involve the children in the planning and making of the roadway.

3. Together, tear pictures of cars and other vehicles from the motoring magazine and stick them to the pieces of thin card. These will be the tickets for using the track.

4. Mark a ticket booth square alongside the track, again with the chalk and masking tape.

5. Play together, with one child in the ticket booth issuing and collecting tickets to and from the children with the wheeled toys as they whizz around the track. You will need a one-way system!

6. Take turns to be in the ticket booth.

7. Use the audible timer to warn the child of changeover time, swapping wheeled toys as well as ticket collector.

Being there – playing, watching, listening, talking

- Warn the children a minute before the timer is about to go.

- Praise turn taking and the swapping of toys.

- Watch the way in which the child with difficulty sharing relates and responds to the other children.

- Consider the different ways they try to get their turn and establish their position within the group of children.

More ideas

- Use a visual warning system of time to stop/swap, such as a black and white checker flag.

- Ring a bell and all the children need to reverse slowly around the track.

- Call 'ticket time', when all the children need to swap their tickets with the child next to them.

Specially for babies

- Find suitable active play and wheeled toys that older babies can share.

- Encourage babies to pull plastic trucks together.

- Build a tower together, taking turns to stack fabric bricks.

Ted's tea party

You first, then me

What you need

- A plastic tea set
- A plastic teapot filled with water
- A tray
- Soft toys

What you do

1. Play alongside the child, taking turns to set out the tea set and pour tea into each cup.

2. Focus on words that define order, such as 'first', 'second', 'third', 'next' and 'last'.

3. Encourage the child to use or imitate simple request phrases, such as 'More tea ted?'.

4. Take one of the soft toys and tell the child that this toy wants his tea now! Encourage the child to explain to the bear, 'doll first, then you' and to reward the waiting bear with 'well done ted, you waited for your tea'.

5. Keep the commentary fun, simple and repetitive.

Being there – playing, watching, listening, talking

- Listen to the language the child uses spontaneously and note the changes in response to your commentary and modelling of appropriate phrases.

- Watch how they respond to other children as they join the activity.

- Note how the play develops and grows according to the child's special interests and current themes.

More ideas

- Brew some different teas. Allow the children to handle and smell the tea leaves, and tear open some tea bags. Allow the brewed tea to cool and then encourage the children to have tiny sips. Again, focus on turn taking and sharing. Give the child you are focusing on the second turn at pouring or tasting.

- Play with the tea set in the water tray, adding plastic food and plates.

- Make some tiny plates for miniature play people and host a small world tea party.

- Encourage the children to work in pairs, spooning and stirring cornflour into water to make gloop. Provide just one spoon and one bowl per pair of children and focus on 'first you' and 'then me' and so on.

Specially for babies

- Sit with two babies and sing a short finger rhyme with one baby and then the next. Again, emphasise 'first *name*, then *name*'.

- Make waiting easier by giving baby something to hold or a special mat to sit on.

- Give specific praise for waiting, and reward with attention and a tickle.

Music and rhyme

Props, prompts and rhythm

What you need

- Help the children to sit in pairs on the floor, opposite each other

- Three bananas, a knife and plate

What you do

1. Sing this rhyme together with the actions (try the tune of the favourite nursery song 'Five currant buns in the baker's shop'):

   Three lovely bananas high up in the tree

   raise arms high

   Ripe and ready for me to eat

   pretend to eat and rub tummy

   Shake, shake, shake and shake the tree

   pretend to shake the tree

   Down they come, one, two, three

   show one, two then three fingers

   One for you and one for me

   outstretch hands towards partner and then touch both hands on own tummy

   And one to save for tea!

   hands together in lap

2. Ask the children to help to peel the bananas. Then slice the bananas and invite another child to offer the fruit around.

Being there – playing, watching, listening, talking

- Encourage the children to feel, smell and taste the fruit.

- Watch to see how the children are able to imitate the actions, show an awareness of their partner and enjoy the actions together.

- Pair more confident children with children less confident or new to this type of activity.

More ideas

- Try this rhyme with apples, plums, oranges and so on.

- Look out for storybooks about sharing and possession, such as *It's My Birthday* by Pat Hutchins (Greenwillow Books). Engage the children's attention with suitable props.

- 'Follow my leader' and similar games for imitating actions and marching bands are all great for encouraging children to feel part of a group and enjoy co-operative play.

Specially for babies

- Look for lift-the-flap books and books with buzzers, strings, textures and so on to explore.

- Finger rhymes are great opportunities to build babies' confidence and develop a shared attention.

- Look out for the 'Amazing Baby' books. They feature wonderfully expressive photographs of babies and a simple repetitive text. Titles include *Baby Boo!*, *Hide and Seek* and *Twinkle Twinkle*. All encourage interactive play and are very engaging for babies and adults alike. These books are widely available online and in high-street book stores.

Pockets and pouches

Using surprise

What you need

- A collection of pretty pouches or small bags.

- Treasure in the form of bits of jewellery, pretty pebbles, old keys, old watches and so on – anything interesting to explore

- Two large baskets

What you do

1. Place one item of treasure in each of the small bags or pouches.

2. Place all the bags in the first basket.

3. Sit opposite the child and you choose one pouch, exploring the contents, showing the treasure to the child and then asking them to return it to the pouch. Then place the explored treasure pouch in the second basket with a firm 'finished'.

4. Offer the remaining pouches to the child to choose just one to explore, share with you and then place in the 'finished' basket.

5. Continue taking turns, keeping to the fixed routine but enjoying the exploration and anticipation of more treasure.

6. When all the pouches have been explored and returned to the 'finished' basket, give the child the opportunity to offer the basket around for other children to explore.

Being there – playing, watching, listening, talking

- Look out for instances of shared attention and note what holds the child's attention.

- Listen to the language they use and how they use it to gain attention.

- Consider what strategies the child is using to help them to wait for their go.

- Are they able to share other children's excitement?

More ideas

- Take turns to dig for buried treasure in the sand tray. Use just one small spade so the children have to take turns and share the spade. Praise good waiting and turn taking.

- Work together to make treasure, pictures and notes to put in small plastic bottles and hide in a garden area. Hunt with other children for the bottles, finding each others' and returning each to the child who created that treasure bottle – an ideal opportunity for 'it's mine'.

- Create a shared treasure basket with each child choosing one item on a theme to go in the basket. Share the contents of the basket in groups or at circle time.

Specially for babies

- Create collections of pairs of identical objects and explore and share these out with two older babies, focusing on 'yours', 'mine', 'same', 'more' and 'all gone'.

- Take turns to explore tokki sticks and other sparkly reflective objects.

- Stand in front of a mirror and place a hat on your head. Shake it off and then put it on the baby's head. Share the fun but focus on 'first me, now you' and so on.

Instant rewards

Using ICT

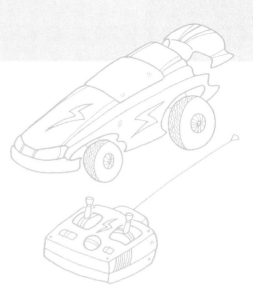

What you need

- A simple battery-operated remote control car or similar

- Chalk or masking tape

- A traffic cone

- Three small cards, each with the number one, two or three on the back

What you do

1. Use the masking tape or chalk to mark a simple roadway leading to the traffic cone. Include a few curves and a starting line.

2. Work with no more than three children, allowing each to explore the operation of the car before starting the game.

3. Place the cards face down and allow each child to choose a number to dictate the order of play.

4. Take turns to steer the car along the track to the traffic cone and back again!

Being there – playing, watching, listening, talking

- Encourage all the children to be involved and shout encouragement to gain a sense of shared attention and to stay in focus even when it is not their go.

- Listen to the children using the language of order of turns: 'first', 'second', 'next', 'last', 'my go next' and so on.

- Praise children when they celebrate other children's successes or offer comfort if cars crash and so on.

More ideas

- Encourage two children to work together at the PC, sharing the keyboard and encouraging and helping each other.

- Play in pairs with a simple timer. Count how many balls each child can throw into a box in 30 seconds and so on.

- Help the children to explore musical keyboards together. Encourage turn taking, finding different pitches of notes, copying rhythms, creating tunes and so on.

Specially for babies

- Look out for simple switch-operated battery toys. They are great for cause and effect as well as turn taking when two babies play together or turn taking between an adult and a baby. Check out your local toy library for a great selection.

- Take turns with the baby, pressing beepers on activity centres and buzzers in activity books. Check out online the 'Tiny Love' range of pull and play activity centres, interactive baby gyms and musical mobiles. For more information about this and other great resources for babies, visit http://toys.nursery-guide.info.

Birthday surprises!

A problem solving circle time

What you need

- A small group of children
- A picture of a bike printed from Google images or torn from the pages of a magazine
- A drawing of a birthday cake with lots of candles on it

What you do

1. Sit with the children in a small circle and remind them of the circle time rules: *sit quietly, listen carefully and say 'pass' if you want to.*

2. Start by passing the cake picture to the first child and prompting them to say, 'I am four years old and on my next birthday I will be five'. This child then passes the cake to the next child in the circle who says, 'I am (so many) years old and on my next birthday...' and so on until the cake has been passed around the circle.

3. Next, explain to the children that there was once a little boy called Tom, who wanted a bike for his birthday, but so did his big sister, Chloe. As he was very lucky, he got a wonderful second-hand bike for his birthday but every time he went outside to play, his sister kept pulling him off it and wouldn't let him enjoy his new bike. Ask the children how Tom might feel. Can the children tell you how his sister is feeling? See if the children can suggest what Tom might be able to do. Remember, it's okay for him to say to his sister, 'This is my bike and I want to play now, but you can have a turn later' and so on.

4. Finish by going around the circle with 'On his next birthday, I would bring Tom a ...'. Encourage the children to choose ridiculous possibilities, such as three elephants, a sky scraper and so on.

5. Thank the children for their ideas, for sitting still and for listening.

Being there – playing, watching, listening, talking

- Listen to the children exploring the ideas of possession and sharing.
- Note if the children relate this game to their own personal experience.
- Watch to see if the children are listening to, and learning from, each other.
- Ask open questions and wonder aloud.
- Be clear that the children all need to sit quietly and listen, and should only speak if they need to.

More ideas

- Look out for toys that need two children to play co-operatively to get them to work together.
- Try some simple skipping-rope play (remember to always supervise the rope and to put it safely away when the activity is finished).
- Encourage the children to paint together at the easel or to create collages together.

Specially for babies

- Play 'pat a cake' with two babies at the same time.
- Encourage two babies to splash their toes in one pool of water at the same time.
- Working opposite another practitioner, gently swing and lift two babies facing each other, whilst dancing and sharing music and song.

Fun with two or three

Working together

What you need

- A large piece of stretchy Lycra fabric
- A beach ball or other soft light ball

What you do

1. Sit on the floor with the children and each grab an edge of the fabric. Pull it tight.

2. Count down 'three, two, one' and then 'GO!' as you let go of the stretched fabric.

3. Each have a go at calling out the countdown and GO as the group stretches and releases the fabric.

4. Next, lay the fabric on the floor and place the ball in the centre. Gently stretch and lift the fabric and then work together to roll the ball around the outstretched cloth without it falling off!

5. Count down together before flipping the soft ball high in the air.

Being there – playing, watching, listening, talking

- Praise the children for working together.

- Ensure all the children get a turn at counting down and also at placing the ball on the Lycra.

- Help the children to encourage and praise each other.

- Think about the praise – use non-verbal signals as well as specific phrases. Does a smile and a thumbs-up work better for some children?

More ideas

- Have a pile of chiffon or light scarves and blow them high in the air together.
- Take one large scarf and all blow hard together. How far will it go?
- Try other co-operative play. Look out for outdoor toys that take two children at a time.
- Help older children to plan and work together to build dens and other imaginative play structures.

Specially for babies

- Soft play is perfect for some gentle turn taking active play.
- Try to borrow a ball pool from your local toy library for some great turn taking active play.

Swap about

Messy play ideas for sharing

What you need

- A shallow tray with the base just covered in gloop (cornflour and water mix)

- Cooked, oiled and cooled spaghetti in another shallow tray

- A plastic box with plastic stirrers, wooden spoons, plastic whisk, small beakers and sieve, and so on

What you do

1. This is seriously messy play with younger children – cover up!

2. Place the two trays opposite each other and encourage the children to choose some stirrers etc. from the plastic box. Allow each child to choose one item and then offer the box to the other child to choose and so on.

3. Sit with the children, talking about the similarities and differences between the utensils, and providing a simple commentary for younger children.

4. Emphasise turn taking, making choices of resources and so on.

5. Encourage the children to swap spoonfuls of materials between the trays.

Being there – playing, watching, listening, talking

- Note the different ways the children negotiate.

- Watch to see if the children are playing entirely solitarily or are aware of playing alongside each other, or actively playing co-operatively together.

- Listen to the ways the children are using language.

- Observe how the children influence each other's exploration of the materials in their tray.

- Encourage lots of swapping and turn taking.

More ideas

- Have two trays full of different coloured jelly and just one empty ice cube tray in the middle. Encourage the children to fill the ice cube tray together with the jellies.

- Play alongside the children as they mix different colours of paint.

- Sit with the children and encourage swapping and turn taking in dressing up.

Specially for babies

- Babies love messy play. Try this activity with cold mashed potato or pumpkin, UHT aerosol cream, chopped-up jelly or sloppy cold custard!

- Explore sound makers together – use lots of hands on one drum and so on.

- Use baby shampoo (no tears shampoo) bubbles on a mirror. Encourage babies to smear the suds around the mirror, patting, wiping and trailing fingers together through the suds.

Shop play
Everyday sharing

What you need

- Shopping bags
- Plastic money and old credit cards
- A calculator
- Lots of packets and pretend food

What you do

1. Involve the children in setting up a shop. Keep it simple with just a few props.

2. Play alongside the children, modelling and helping with queues, waiting turns to shop and swapping roles, such as shopkeeper, shelf stacker, shopper and so on.

3. Talk to each shopper about what they have bought. Encourage the children to show an interest in each other's shopping.

Being there – playing, watching, listening, talking

- Help the children to make choices. Encourage orderly queuing and the taking of turns!

- Play with the children, prompting scenarios where two children want to buy the last apple and so on.

- Listen to the language the children are using related to sharing and possession.

- Note how the children respond to the model of earlier customers.

More ideas

- Set up a shoe shop. This is great for opportunities for measuring, matching and sorting as well as making choices and taking turns.

- Set up a pizza parlour. Use cardboard pizzas cut from the front of pizza boxes. Cut some up into slices. Create menus together and encourage children to order.

- Post office play offers lots of opportunities for shop play, sharing, handing out letters and parcels as well as taking turns with central roles, such as delivering letters, behind the counter and so on.

Specially for babies

- Create a treasure basket of interesting parcels and packages for babies to explore.

- Take turns to post objects into a box.

- Take babies on shopping trips and encourage them to place fruit and packets into the shopping basket.

Advice

Some early experiences, such as the arrival of a new baby, starting at a new setting, changing to a new group or key person, or changes of routine at home can all be factors in a child's need for extra time and input to enable them to overcome difficulties in sharing. We have all heard shouts of, 'now', 'mine' and 'I want it now'! When children do experience strong emotions and portray some of the behaviours listed above, practitioners can do much to help.

Tips for practitioners when faced with a distraught child:

- Use a calm quiet voice.

- Get down to the child's eye level.

- Be careful to present open, friendly body language.

- Use the child's name first to grab their attention.

- Work to gain the child's trust and then ask them to give you (or put in a safe place) the disputed item. It should stay there whilst you negotiate sharing and turn taking with them and other children involved in the dispute.

- Prompt and praise at every stage.

- Ask even very young children to suggest a solution.

- Praise the child (or children) for finding a solution.

Remember that as feelings will be running high, the children will be so focused on the disputed object that they will have difficulty listening. Give both children equal attention. Do not tolerate children hurting each other in any way.

Be sure to find a fun activity later for the children to share with each other – review together what has been learnt about sharing and the positive strategy agreed. Praise children for waiting patiently, being kind, speaking quietly, listening to the other child and so on – focus on all the positive attributes you wish to nurture.

By helping a child who struggles with sharing and turn taking, assisting them to understand possession and respect others, you will be providing that child with the building blocks of positive relationships with other children. This will enable them to play and learn co-operatively as part of a group and, most importantly, experience the joy of sharing in the successes and pleasures of others.

Losing It!
Managing anger

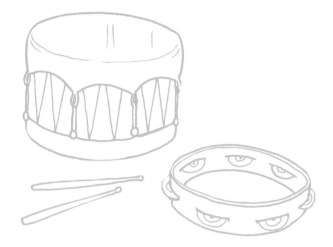

Contents

Introduction

Feeling angry and losing your temper are perfectly natural parts of everyday life, and many children cope well when they feel angry, but for some children, feelings of anger can get out of control. How children understand and express their emotions and adapt to their new life depends on many factors including their:

- developmental stage

- position in their family and the attention they are used to

- relationship with key people in their life

- opportunities to communicate their anger and frustration

- the response they get from others

- learning strategies for managing their emotions

- the models they get of adults and other children managing strong feelings without getting out of control.

Feeling angry is a completely natural and reasonable emotional response to some circumstances. Anger tends to be thought of in very negative terms and from a very early age children are encouraged to try and hold this anger in. Adults and children can expend enormous amounts of energy holding anger in, but anger can be a very positive dynamic emotion, giving us strength and focus to overcome difficult challenges. Problems occur when anger is expressed inappropriately. From the beginning children need to understand that it is natural to have strong feelings, that feeling angry is okay, but that it is not okay to be hurtful because they feel angry.

Children need to learn how to take charge of their angry feelings, and to recognise that there are three clearly defined stages to feeling angry:

1. The first trigger – the thing that made them cross (for example when they have to wait or take turns);

2. A physical response to the anger (maybe shouting, hitting, sulking or throwing a tantrum);

3. Understanding what has happened and resolving it (recognising emotions and knowing how to take charge of feelings).

What you might see and what the child might be feeling

Every child and every set of circumstances is unique, but young children are far more likely to show us how they are feeling long before they are able to understand what they are feeling or tell us.

A child may express their anger in many different ways, some very obvious, others less so. Some of these signs and behaviours might be:

- tantrums

- hitting or biting

- relapse in toilet training

- tearfulness or anger

- hurting themselves

- withdrawing

- crying or sulking

- teasing or bullying other children.

A child might be feeling any or all of these:

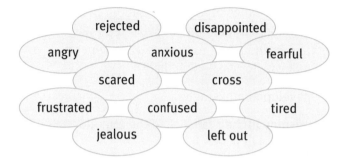

Practitioners should be mindful of any changes in a child's behaviour, observe the child carefully and discuss the child's needs together, taking note of what others in the team have observed or heard.

Puddle stomp
Stamping and chanting

What you need

- Big boots
- Huge socks
- Funny slippers
- Sheets of bubble wrap

What you do

1. Help the child to spread the bubble wrap out on the floor. Use the masking tape to secure the edges.

2. Have a look at the boots, socks and slippers together and let the child choose some for you to wear and then some for themselves.

3. Hold hands and together start stamping about on the bubble wrap.

4. After a little while, let the child take the lead with you following their actions.

5. Chant or sing a commentary, such as 'Stamp, stamp, STAMP, stamp, stamp STAMP' or 'Jump, jump JUMP'.

6. Tell them how this can sometimes help with angry feelings. Continue stamping and jumping together.

7. Swap over and try the other footwear. Try and bring the conversation round to feelings. Talk about what you can do when you are feeling cross or angry inside. Reassure the child that when they are feeling cross they can tell you or come and get the bubble wrap out for a good stamp around.

Being there – playing, watching, listening, talking

- Let the child take the lead with the actions and talking. Listen carefully without interrupting, repeating what the child says back to them using their own words to show that you are really listening.

- Give the child plenty of time to get into this activity. They may want to just sit and pop the bubbles first. It takes time to have the confidence to really let go of feelings.

- Make time at the end of the activity to have some quiet time together, this gives them time to calm down as well as time to say anything they might want to say.

More ideas

- Pull on some waterproof clothing and waterproof boots and stamp in real puddles.

- Take off your shoes and socks and stand on wet grass together for a few moments. Breathe deeply and look at the plants, trees and clouds.

- Move into a safe space with a soft bean bag. Take off socks and shoes and take turns to give it a good kick.

Specially for babies

- Make a pat mat from some squidgy sponge and take turns to pat it hard.

- Find some really sturdy shakers and make a BIG noise together.

- Inflate a beach ball so that it's still soft. Encourage the baby to hit or kick at the ball in a safe place.

Big box bash

Take it out on a box!

What you need

- Newspaper

- Several different sizes of cardboard boxes (check there are no staples in them)

- Cardboard tubes from the inside of kitchen rolls

- Masking tape

What you do

1. Spend some time together really scrunching up large sheets of old newspaper. Make long twisted shapes and scrunchy balls.

2. Encourage the child to throw the scrunched up paper into the boxes.

3. Bash the boxes with twisted paper wands and cardboard tubes. Try to really flatten them onto the floor. Stamp on the boxes.

4. Work together to press as much screwed-up paper as possible into one of the boxes. Climb in the box and jump on the paper to press it down. Then press down the lid together really hard and seal it with masking tape.

5. Talk about how you feel now you have worked so hard and how much energy you must have used. Talk about how using lots of energy and taking lots of exercise can change feelings and moods, making you feel better when you are cross or upset.

Being there – playing, watching, listening, talking

- Reassure the child that such boisterous play is okay as long as no-one is getting hurt.

- Make sure you have enough time for the child to finish the activity in their own time and plan for a cooling off time. You could wash your hands together in luke-warm water and spend a few minutes carefully drying the child's hands and massaging in a tiny drop of baby oil or moisturiser.

More ideas

- Vigorous exercise is a great way to get angry feelings under control. Offer a small trampoline, or put the boxes on a safe surface and help them to jump up and down on them until they are satisfyingly flattened.

- Play together in some very damp sand. Use just hands to fill sand moulds. Tip them out and flatten them by splatting them with your hands. Do some yourself to show the child that it's okay to use such force in a safe way.

Specially for babies

- Build an oasis or special calm place for the baby to retreat to when angry.

- For older babies and very young children, stitch a smiley face to one side of a floor cushion and a sad face on the other side of the floor cushion. Let the child choose which side they want to curl up on.

Bean bag boxer

Use that energy!

What you need

- A big bean bag or floor cushion
- Small hand-held bean bags
- Two smaller cushions

What you do

1. Sit alongside the child, each of you on a cushion on the floor.

2. Share the small bean bags out between you and place the large bean bag or a floor cushion about one metre away.

3. Take turns to throw the small bean bags rapidly at the target bean bag seat and as soon as they are all thrown, encourage the child to belly flop or dive into the large bean bag cushion with them.

4. Have another go!

5. Comment on how you feel when you have done this, Such as 'I was feeling really cross before we played this game because I had lost my keys but now I feel a little better'.

6. Pause to allow time for the child to respond. Invite them to play again, but this time try to throw even faster.

Being there – playing, watching, listening, talking

- Playing alongside and joining in, and sharing your thoughts and feelings all help towards building rapport and gaining the child's trust – both are vital if they are going to be able to express their feelings, and for you to gain an insight into why they might be feeling so angry.

- Allow plenty of time to respond, with many quiet pauses.

- Be sure to finish the game with a quiet relaxing time – perhaps some favourite finger rhymes – together on the bean bag seat.

More ideas

- Find some washing up sponges that are fixed to plastic handles. Dip these in soapy water and beat them on the ground or on upturned plastic buckets and boxes.

- Digging is a great way to get rid of anger and frustration. Try and create a digging area in your setting.

- Roll lots and lots of small play dough balls for the child to squish. Dough play can be very calming.

Specially for babies

- Give babies a bowl or tray of jelly to squish, grasp and pat. Imitate their actions.

- Gently rock babies and young children in a strong blanket from side to side as you sing a soothing rhythmic nursery song.

- Provide older babies and very young children with carefully supervised shallow ball pool play.

Perfect pizza

Get rid of frustration – make a pizza

What you need

- Pizza dough packet mix
- Aprons
- Ripe tomatoes, skinned and cooled
- Grated cheese
- Baking tray
- Warm water
- Rolling pin

What you do

1. Wash hands together, using the opportunity to talk about cooking or meals at home.

2. Explain that you feel the child could be a really good chef and you would love them to help you make some pizza treats for all the other children.

3. Put on aprons. Ask the child to help you fasten your apron and ask if you can help fasten theirs.

4. Make up the pizza dough together, according to the packet instructions. Take time kneading the dough and talking together. Explain that you really enjoy cooking and that it makes you happy. Ask the child what sorts of things make them happy.

5. Divide the dough into small bite size pizzas for the other children in the setting, and talk about the child's friendships.

6. Squeeze the peeled tomatoes through your fingers and a sieve. Spread the tomato pulp onto the pizza tops.

7. Add grated cheese to each bite and then bake the mini pizzas as per instructions, then invite the other children to try the pizzas, praising the child who made them.

Being there – playing, watching, listening, talking

- Getting really absorbed in this sort of activity helps an angry child to calm down, and they may also be able to express their feelings more easily when they are focused on a creative but structured process.

- Model words that describe feelings. This helps the child to realise that everyone sometimes experiences intense emotions but also gives them the language to process their own feelings. It is important to acknowledge emotions. Try saying, 'You look like you might be feeling angry. Is something upsetting you?', or 'You look like you're feeling happy/sad'.

More ideas

- Beating simple cake mix and creaming butter and flour together by hand are both very tactile activities that can be totally absorbing, calming and special.

- Help the child to use a hand whisk with some soapy water to make lots and lots of bubbles and suds.

- Try a bubble machine to make hundreds of bubbles to play in and catch. This is good to do outside.

Specially for babies

- A bowl full of cooked pasta tossed in a couple of drops of olive oil is a soothing and satisfying finger play activity.

- Gently brush warm water with a small clean soft paint brush over the baby's hands. Do this slowly and sing a gentle commentary to the child as you play.

Big band
Make a big sound

What you need

- Two tambourines
- Two drums
- Two beaters
- Some marching music. For a great selection of music for early years settings, go to: www.kidsmusiceducation.com

What you do

1. Listen to the marching music together and practise marching and stamping around outside.

2. Sit opposite each other. Play a simple game of 'Follow my leader' with the drums and beaters. Imitate the child's actions carefully and more quietly than they are beating.

3. Next, place the tambourines on the ground next to the drum. Work together to set up a steady beat. Beat the drum on the first beat, and the tambourine on the second beat. One, two, one, two, and so on.

4. Talk about how you are feeling after the drumming session. Give the child an opportunity to tell you how they are feeling.

5. Spend a little time together exploring how to make quiet sounds on the drum and tambourine as a calming end to this activity.

Being there – playing, watching, listening, talking

- Set aside enough uninterrupted time for the child to be able to take the lead on this activity and enjoy your close attention.

- If the child appears uncomfortable, sit alongside them rather than opposite.

- This is a great activity for enjoying your individual attention and lots of action without the need for the child to talk.

More ideas

- Suspend lots of sturdy everyday objects from a simple frame. Play alongside the child hitting the objects with a beater or stick.

- Make a really big shaker by putting plastic bricks inside a cardboard box and sealing it. Roll it around outside for some vigorous noisy play.

- Put some headphones and a simple music player in a small tented area with some cushions for a quiet zone.

Specially for babies

- Try some simple banging of pots and pans with a metal spoon.

- Look out for wobble toys that fix with strong suction cups to trays. They are great for some really strong pushing and pulling – a good way to get all the frustration out.

Rip and stick

Cover it all with layers and layers

What you need

- Old newspapers
- Paste in a small bucket
- Large decorating paint brushes
- Big pens
- Large sheet of paper

What you do

1. On the large sheet of paper start to draw pictures and simple symbols of things that make you feel angry/sad/disappointed. Invite the child to add their ideas and draw their own pictures on the same sheet of paper.

2. Together tear lots of really long strips of newspaper. As you work, chat about the sorts of things you could do to calm yourself when you have angry feelings.

3. Use the big paint brushes to apply lots of paste to the picture and stick the lengths of newsprint criss cross over the picture.

4. Build up lots of layers. Add any extra pictures, words and symbols to the picture that the child suggests as you play. They will need plenty of time to think about the sorts of things that make them angry.

5. Reassure the child that it's okay to feel angry and that sometimes we don't know why we feel angry. Talk to the child about why it's important to tell someone how you are feeling, so they can help you handle those angry feelings to feel calmer and happier.

Being there – playing, watching, listening, talking

- How much a child can tell you about how they are feeling through words, actions or body language will depend on how much they trust you to handle their feelings calmly. This will take time, particularly if the child has had experience of their feelings being dismissed.

- Listen carefully. Sometimes the silences and pauses tell you more than the words used by a child. Observe body language carefully so that you can respond sensitively to the child.

More ideas

- Chalk boards and wet chalks are a good way to make strong marks to convey feelings that are easily wiped away if the child wishes to erase them.

- Try drawing in wet sand or offering some clay play. Both provide strong sensory feedback to the child which can be particularly rewarding and comforting to a distressed child.

Specially for babies

- Check out 'Baby and Beyond: Messy Play'(Featherstone), for lots of calming messy play ideas for babies and very young children.

- Make sure that the child has their comfort toy easily and readily available. Keep the comfort toys of more mobile children in a safe place you can easily find them.

Squeeze it!

Sudsy water for outside play

What you need

- Washing up bowl
- Warm soapy water
- Different textured wash cloths and flannels
- Different sizes of sponges
- Plastic containers and cups

What you do

1. Sit with the child and explore all the different cloths and sponges. How tight can you wring them or squeeze them? How small can you scrunch them up? Can you squeeze them into containers or cups?

2. Talk about how you feel as you play. Mention what you like about the activity and how it makes you feel.

3. Listen to the child's comments and watch quietly as they play, observing their body language and non-verbal communication.

4. Take the bowl outside and play at throwing the wet cloths and sponges – splat them onto the ground. Wash them in the bowl, wring them out and do it again.

5. When you have finished, tip the bubbly water on the ground or the grass and stamp or paddle in it.

Being there – playing, watching, listening, talking

- When you see a strong emotion in the child, acknowledge this by saying 'You look like you might be feeling sad/angry now, what can we do to help?'. Comment also on your own feelings when you are relaxed, tired, hot, hungry, thirsty or even angry.

- Think about the child's experience in the setting. Are there ways you could provide more choices, more 'down' time, more routine or structure for the child? Talk it through with the child's parents and key person in the setting.

More ideas

- Make a squeezy basket – a collection of toys for squeezing and pulling. Try koosh balls, bits of Lycra fabric, play putty and so on.

- Take off some cushion covers together. Spend time stuffing the cushions back in and plumping them up.

- Hang a small rug over a washing line and try some old fashioned carpet beating. Make sure the other children stay at a safe distance!

Specially for babies

- Spread some bubbly suds on a safety mirror and play at patting the foam.

- Rubbery squeezy squeakers need a big action and create a big noise – very satisfying if you are small and cross!

Hammer away
Pounding and beating

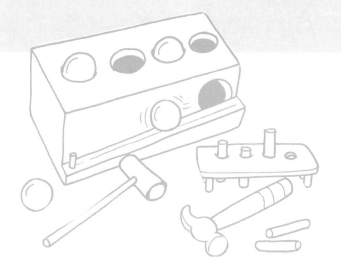

What you need

- A bag of plastic golf tees
- A child sized play plastic hammer
- Lots of clean egg boxes

What you do

1. Sit together and show the child how to hammer the golf tees into the upside down egg boxes. Show the child how to use the hammer safely.

2. Let the child enjoy the hammering. If they seem relaxed, take the opportunity to mention that sometimes we all have different feelings and that's good, as long as we don't get so upset that we lose control. Encourage the child to talk about when they might experience strong emotions.

3. Reflect back what they say, acknowledging their feelings and reassuring them that having those feelings is okay. Give a simple example of when you had the same emotion, explain why and what action you took to manage that feeling.

4. Sing 'Johnny hammers with one hammer' together as you hammer more pegs into the egg boxes or into a big block of polystyrene or firm sponge.

Being there – playing, watching, listening, talking

- Enjoy a few minutes of shared attention on this simple and satisfying activity.

- Model appropriate language to express feelings. Observe the child carefully as you talk and listen to them. Actions and body language are the way many young children tell us how they are feeling.

- Make sure the child has unconditional positive regard – that they know you like them, even if you do not always like their actions or behaviour.

More ideas

- Set up a simple tool shop with a plastic play tool set for lots of hammering opportunities.

- Sing lots of action songs and rhymes to get rid of feelings, and march, stamp and jump as you sing. For lots more construction related songs and action rhymes visit www.prekfun.com

Specially for babies

- Offer the baby two small balls to bang together.

- Pop some children's sized novelty gloves on the baby's hands and play simple tapping and clapping games together.

- Finish vigorous activities with a quiet hug, a favourite rhyme and a look at a picture book together.

An oasis

Creating a safe place

What you need

- A big cardboard box
- Cushions and bean bags
- A soft blanket
- Lightweight fabrics
- Clips or pegs
- String

What you do

1. The aim is to create a calm, quiet, uncluttered space where a child who is feeling tired, fearful, anxious, overwhelmed or angry can retreat to rest, think and watch. This will be different in every setting. It may be as simple as a cosy armchair with big cushions, or a small tented area with a soft blanket and cushion. Choose calm colours and plain fabrics if possible. Think about the textures and smells that a child will encounter.

2. Position the oasis so that a child can be easily seen by adults without having to intrude on their quiet time, as well as enabling the child to watch what is happening in the setting without getting actively involved.

3. Why not add a cushion with a smiley face on one side and a sad face on the other? Some children might choose to use this to say how they are feeling.

4. It's important that the child's key person lets the child quietly know with a reassuring smile, touch or nod that they are aware that the child has chosen to spend a few moments in the oasis.

Being there – playing, watching, listening, talking

- You need to balance enabling the child to retreat and the child knowing that their key person is available to comfort or be alongside them if they wish. Watch and use your judgement and knowledge of the child.

- Observe carefully and plan different ways the child can convey their feelings – paper and pens for drawings and mark making, choosing sticky labels with different faces etc.

More ideas

- Add a lavender pillow or place a few drops of lavender oil on a small pillow or cushion in the oasis.

- Introduce a special soft toy that loves to be cuddled. Make a special place for it to sit. Keep it away from everyday play but easily accessible to the children should they want to give it a quiet hug anytime.

Specially for babies

- Try a simple very gentle baby hands and feet massage using just a tiny drop of baby oil.

- Curl up together with a tape of soothing relaxing music. See suggestions in the resources section.

A bit of calm

Soothing, calming play

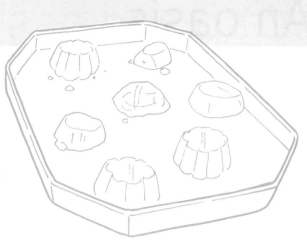

What you need

- Packet jelly made up in ice cube trays and turned out on a shallow tray

- Lolly sticks

- Small buttons, beads

What you do

1. Sit together and gently poke and prod the jelly with your finger tips. Use a quiet calm voice to provide a simple commentary to describe what you are doing together.

2. Slow down your actions and words to create a calming atmosphere. Explore the jelly, how it feels, smells, and the way it changes as it is pushed, poked and prodded.

3. Offer the child a lolly stick to prod and smear the jelly. Push the buttons and beads into the jelly.

4. Play slowly and gently. Comment on how calming and relaxing this activity can be. Invite the child to tell you which activities they like, which make them feel excited and which give a calm feeling.

5. Talk about calm feelings at home as well as in the setting.

6. Finish the session by tipping the jelly into some warm water and swishing it round till it melts and disappears.

Being there – playing, watching, listening, talking

- Try and influence the child's mood by being especially calm and relaxed.

- Make sure you are sitting at their level for easy eye contact. Sit alongside the child rather than opposite the child for calm and non-confrontational interaction.

- Be confident in just playing alongside, without feeling that you need to say anything or challenge the child in any way. Just being there and relaxing alongside the child will help them gain a sense of peace.

More ideas

- Stand together and watch clouds moving across the sky, or follow raindrops as they trickle down windows.

- Play simple clapping games together. They are a great way to make a connection with a child that is calming down after feeling very angry. For more clapping game ideas, try Baby and Beyond: Finger Songs and Rhymes (Featherstone Education).

Specially for babies

- Many babies find being wrapped in a light, soft sheet soothing.

- Think about the environment. Is the baby being over-stimulated? Perhaps a gentle hug as you walk around outside for a few minutes is all they need.

Wrap and pass

Wrapping up tiny notes

What you need

- Sheets of old newspaper
- Tiny bits of paper
- Pens
- Sticky or masking tape
- 'Pumpkin Soup' by Helen Cooper, or another picture story book that encourages talk about feelings.

What you do

1. Read the book 'Pumpkin Soup' together.

2. Talk about the sorts of feelings that the main characters experience, and encourage talk about what triggered those feelings.

3. Talk about and draw some of those feelings on tiny bits of paper. Ask the child to draw pictures of their own feelings and add some of your own.

4. Wrap all the tiny bits of paper up in a sheet of newspaper and secure with tape. Let the child add a second layer. Take turns and help each other to add lots of layers.

5. Keep talking about how the story characters handled their feelings and how they might have managed them.

6. Next, encourage the child to rip off all the layers of paper!

7. Fetch a rubbish bin and have a race to get all the bits of paper in the bin. Letting them win would be tactful!

Being there – playing, watching, listening, talking

- Ask open questions that encourage the child to talk without probing.
- Watch their body language carefully so that you can respond appropriately.
- Use humour to gently diffuse any difficult moments, but be aware of the children who are just made worse by this response!

More ideas

- Take time to paint together at the easel.
- Make the child feel important and special but be sure to do this when they are calm and not as a reward for actions that are an inappropriate way to express angry feelings.
- Share some of the story books from the resources section together. They all provide good opportunities to talk about feelings in a safe way.

Specially for babies

- Babies can be comforted and reassured by familiar smells and textures. Make sure that the baby's comfort object or favourite soft toy is always available.
- Try whispering to a baby who is distressed, or blow gently on their fingers and toes.

A hundred tiny pieces
Letting go of emotions

What you need

- Small pieces of paper
- Pens
- Two envelopes

What you do

1. Fold small bits of paper in half to make some small cards.

2. Talk to the child and on the front of each card help them to draw or make a symbol to represent a 'feeling face' – happy, sad, angry, disappointed etc.

3. Talk together and inside each card draw a simple picture to say what can cause that feeling, for example for a 'feeling cross face' there could be a picture of a broken toy inside. Make sure you acknowledge any feelings and causes the child describes as real and as equally important as your contributions and feelings.

4. Help the child to sort the cards into two envelopes, one of good feelings to keep and one of bad feelings to tear up.

5. Tear the bad feelings envelope up into lots and lots of tiny pieces.

6. If you can face the mess, throw all the tiny pieces of paper up in the air and let the draught blow the bad feelings away.

Being there – playing, watching, listening, talking

- Encourage the child to think about what triggers their feelings. Talk about what they might do and who can help them to cope with their feelings.

- Reassure the child that it's good to have strong feelings and praise them for times when they have managed their feelings appropriately.

- Make a special tiny smiley face picture and give it to the child to keep in their pocket for the rest of the day. Reward them for talking and listening.

More ideas

- Give the child who is feeling angry lots and lots of specific praise. Give lots of reassurance, thumbs up signs, nods and smiles. If anger is expressed in an inappropriate way, be specific, use positive language that explains what they could have done differently but soon after, find them behaving appropriately and start praising them again. Be sure to talk all this through with parents as this method needs a consistent approach.

Specially for babies

- Use simple repetitive language to help babies and very young children develop situational understanding. Remember that most babies prefer routine to surprises.

Advice

Some tips for practitioners:

- Watch for the triggers – they may be different for different children.

- Note what happened just before the outburst – this is often a clue, particularly if it's the same thing every time – Mum leaving, a change of routine, a particular activity.

- Always respond calmly and quietly.

- Remove the child from any dangers, such as objects they might bump into or things they might throw.

- Remove other children from the area – an audience sometimes makes things worse!

- Avoid discussion at this stage, just wait for the temper to subside a bit before trying to reason with them.

- Some children respond well to being held while they calm down, others hate it – find out what works best for the individual.

- Acknowledge their feelings of frustration and anger in your expression and words.

- Comfort any children who may have been innocently caught up in the event.

- Provide an understanding and supportive environment.

- Use books and stories to help children understand their emotions.

- Find ways for the child to express their anger appropriately.

- Offer activities that provide a physical outlet for the child's anger through vigorous exercise and play.

- Develope a safe space or oasis to be calm.

- Be an effective listener and observer, responding to their needs.

- Encourage empathy and understanding in other children and staff.

Some tips to share with parents:

Parents can help their child to deal with frustration and angry outbursts by:

- keeping calm

- if the child is angry, keeping words to a minimum, but acknowledging the child's feelings

- acknowledging the child's feelings by saying, 'I know you feel cross but we need to take turns/get the shopping/only have sweets at the weekend' etc.

- quietly telling the child what they need to do to calm down, 'You need to take a deep breath' (or another calming device)

- staying with the child, while remaining calm

- distracting the child before they get frustrated or angry

- making lots of short opportunities for the child to rest and relax with the parent while you are with them – don't rush about!

- offering plenty of drinks and lots of fresh air and exercise – avoid over stimulating a child at the end of a long busy day

- making time at the end of every day to talk about the day gives the child the chance to ask questions or have a much needed extra hug

- keeping in mind that taking charge of angry feelings comes with time and maturity. Understanding child development will provide insight into why children have difficulty expressing their emotions

- trying to be a good role model. Children look to the most important people in their life and try to imitate their behaviour

- trying out some of the ideas in this book. They use everyday objects and are easy and quick to do.

I Can't Do It!

Building confidence

Contents

Introduction

Feeling less confident and unable to tackle new things are perfectly natural parts of everyday life, and many children cope well when they feel lacking in confidence – they have a 'can do' attitude. But for some children, confidence and self-esteem are so low that they may refuse to even try and may resort to tears, withdrawal or even tantrums. How children understand and express their emotions and adapt to their new life depends on many factors including their:

- developmental stage

- position in their family and the attention they are used to

- relationship with key people in their life

- the response they get from others

- learning strategies for managing their emotions

- opportunities to communicate their feelings of self-esteem

- the models they get of adults and other children managing strange feelings without getting out of control.

Gaining self-esteem and confidence is difficult, particularly if this has been eroded by early failure, lack of response or 'learned helplessness', where a baby or child is over-protected or not given the freedom to 'have a go'. In these cases it is important for practitioners and parents to work together to restore the confidence which is normally present in early childhood.

Children need to learn how to take charge of their feelings, and to recognise:

- making mistakes is part of everyday life, and is not failure

- learning something new usually needs several attempts and some concentration

- everyone has strengths and also things they find difficult, and we all feel insecure and less confident sometimes.

What you might see and what the child might be feeling

Every child and every set of circumstances is unique, but young children are far more likely to show us how they are feeling long before they are able to understand what they are feeling or tell us.

A child may express their lack of confidence in many different ways, some very obvious, others less so. Some of these signs and behaviours might be:

- crying, sulking or refusing to try an activity
- extreme stillness
- relapse in toilet training
- hiding or turning away from contact
- throwing things or tantrums
- violence to other children and adults.

A child might be feeling any or all of these:

Practitioners should be mindful of any changes in a child's behaviour, observe the child carefully and discuss the child's needs together, taking note of what others in the team have observed or heard.

Easy marks

Making marks that disappear

What you need

- Decorating paintbrushes
- Seaside buckets or plastic boxes of water

What you do

1. This activity helps children to become confident about mark making, as the marks can be erased easily or left to disappear on their own. Start with just water.

2. Go outside with your buckets and brushes and see what you can paint.

3. You can use water on outdoor furniture, on the walls and doors, on climbing apparatus and on the ground. As you paint together, talk about how the water changes the colours of the things you are painting.

4. Watch the marks as they dry and disappear. Try making some letter-like marks or writing your name and then watching it disappear. Talk about the fun of making marks that don't matter. You can make them as big and sloppy as you like. Encourage the child to make really big arm and body movements as they work, reaching to the top of walls and doors, and making big circles and lines. Use plenty of praise for effort.

5. Tip the rest of the water out and sit together to watch it spread out and disappear.

Being there – playing, watching, listening, talking

- Watch for anything you can notice and praise – shapes, movements and design, or just having a go. Help them to relax by suggesting that you make really big arm movements and shapes.

- Get involved yourself. Modelling confidence is very important, and children love it if you get involved.

- Offer this activity as a permanent feature of your setting, it's a great confidence builder for all children, and helps with hand control for writing later.

More ideas

- Put a bit of washing up liquid in the water for bubbly painting, or add some food colouring.

- Put bubbly water in washing up bowls or bigger containers and offer the children small brooms so they can paint on an even bigger scale.

- Put up a big blackboard outside for water painting or use small blackboards and cotton buds.

Specially for babies

- Make some pat mats from zip lock bags with coloured water or cellulose paste mixed with food colouring inside. Let the babies pat these bags with dry or wet hands.

- Mix some soapy foam or use non-allergenic shaving foam in shallow dishes for patting and poking.

- Help them make marks in finger paint or custard.

Higher and higher

Building towers

What you need

- Big building blocks
- A child's hard hat
- An adult hard hat (if possible)
- A camera

What you do

1. Bricks are meant to be built and knocked over. Use this game to help a child understand that they have control over the structures they make, and that knocking them down can be good fun too.

2. Sit together with the bricks, wearing hard hats to get in the mood, and build towers and structures.

3. Talk about the towers you are building, counting the bricks and knocking your own towers down, or inviting the child to knock down your towers. Ask them if they can build a tower and knock it down themselves.

4. Build some very tall towers together, count '1, 2, 3, GO!' and let the child knock them down.

5. It may take some time before the child will build a tower and let you knock it down! Be patient as they gain confidence in building and demolishing.

6. Play the game with all sorts of bricks and towers indoors and outside.

Being there – playing, watching, listening, talking

- Watch the child's face as they build the towers and knock them down again. Are they anxious? Do they get over-excited as you count and knock them down? Do they ask you to do it? Are they happy to build it up again? Praise their efforts.

- Show your enjoyment as the bricks come tumbling down. Talk as you build and demolish – say that you are going to build the highest tower you can, so you can make a big crash.

More ideas

- Use smaller bricks and knock them down with toy bulldozers and diggers.

- Use Duplo, Stickle Bricks and other construction sets to make structures that can be knocked down deliberately. This will strengthen their confidence in trying different sorts of towers and not getting upset when they fall.

- Make dough balls and pile these up before knocking them down or squishing them.

Specially for babies

- Sit with a baby and pile up soft bricks on a flat floor, taking turns to put one on top of another and enjoying the falling down. Praise their efforts in building and demolishing!

- Stick construction pieces, such as Duplo or Stickle Bricks together for them to pull apart again.

Look what I can do

A photo book

What you need

- Child's digital camera
- Scissors
- A piece of ribbon or string
- Pieces of card or stiff paper
- Glue stick
- Hole punch

What you do

1. Talk with the child and suggest that you make a 'can-do' photo book with pictures of all the things they can do. They could tell you the things they can do and you could make a simple list. Add to this with things you know the child can do. If they are feeling very lacking in confidence, they may need help from you. Walk around your setting reminding them of the things they like to do and do well, but don't go on too long.

2. Collect the things you need to make the book.

3. Talk about the camera and how it works. Decide who will take the photos. The child could photograph the resources and equipment or you could photograph them doing things. Let them decide, they may not want you to take pictures of them.

4. Take the photos or help them to. Try to look at the outdoor area as well as indoors, physical activities, friends, favourite places, personal qualities.

5. Print the photos and look at them together as you stick them on small sheets of card.

6. Help the child to punch holes in each card and thread the ribbon through to tie it.

7. Decorate the cover together and write the child's name on it.

8. Don't forget to show the book to the child's parents and the other children.

Being there – playing, watching, listening, talking

- Take special note of the things the child feels really confident about – the first things they say they can do. These will be useful starting points if difficulties arise in the future.

- As you work, talk about the things the child likes doing, things you like doing, and things that are hard to do. Recognise that everyone finds some things hard to do, and that practice is important, because you don't always get it right first time.

More ideas

- If you do something new, such as passing your driving test, getting a new qualification, learning to swim, cooking a new recipe, talk about it with the children – how you had to practise and how pleased and proud you are now you can do it.

- Make an achievement tree or wall for the whole group, and add a leaf or brick with a photo when a child learns to do something new.

Specially for babies

- Remember to give babies plenty of time to practise new skills. Praise them when they keep trying, talk about what they are doing, and make positive comments when they achieve something new.

- Talk to parents about their baby's achievements, and give praise for new skills learned.

I think I can

Using stories to build confidence

What you need

- A story from the resources section or one you already have
- A familiar puppet or soft toy

What you do

1. There are lots of stories about being persistent and trying again. Choose one from your own setting or buy a few titles to keep handy for these times.

2. Don't worry if the story isn't an exact match with the activity the child is finding difficult, in some ways it will make it easier to discuss. Stories with animal characters are often more successful than ones about other children.

3. Read the story together and talk about how the character in the story felt and how they overcame their problem, who helped them and what they did.

4. Now introduce the soft toy or puppet. Tell the child their name and say that they have a problem too. At this point you could choose to talk about another problem or the one the child is currently facing – for example, 'Do you know, Malcolm said he wasn't very good at drawing, and so he wouldn't try, and he got very upset when his friends were drawing and he wanted to do it too. How can we help him?'

5. Encourage the child to think of ways to help the toy, and this will help them to think about strategies for themselves, so next time they face the problem, they can think about the toy or puppet, they may even like to hold it to help them feel more confident.

Being there – playing, watching, listening, talking

- Listen carefully to the child's comments and suggestions, take these seriously, and use them to help you understand what the child is feeling.

- If the child uses one of the strategies later, praise them for remembering what to do.

- When the difficult challenge happens again, gently remind them of the story or the character, and perhaps put the book or toy where the child can see them as they work or play.

More ideas

- Use a wooden train set to retell the story, making up a tune or chanting 'I think I can, I think I can' as the train goes over the track.

- Circle time is a good time to raise children's worries, concerns and difficulties. Give the children plenty of time to volunteer themselves, but don't force them or name them to others.

Specially for babies

- If babies feel less confident, they will usually respond if you give them some more of your time. Watch them carefully and give plenty of encouragement.

- When a baby shows signs of insecurity and lack of confidence, talk to their parents or carers and try to find out if anything has happened at home to trigger the worry.

I can make it work

Technology that works

What you need

- A children's CD player
- Some CDs of quiet music or stories
- A quiet place to listen
- A big cushion or bean bag

What you do

1. Sit with the child in a quiet, comfortable place and look at the CD player together. Show them how it works.

2. Let them have a turn at pressing the buttons and turning the knobs. Give them plenty of praise for having a go. You could take a photo to show their parents how clever they are!

3. Try some different CDs and let the child choose which one they want to listen to. Sit comfortably together and listen to some quiet music or a story. You could fetch a teddy or soft toy to share the quiet time with you.

4. Let the child stop the machine when they want to talk or change the CD. Don't make them listen for longer than they want. It's working the machine and being in control that's important – this improves confidence and self-esteem.

5. Stop when they have had enough. Don't forget to let them tell other adults and children what they have done. Prompt them if they need support in doing this.

Being there – playing, watching, listening, talking

- Watch the child's level of confidence in different activities. They may be very confident with handling equipment, but not so good at telling people what they can do. They may be good at talking but not very good at listening. Make sure you know each child well, and can use their strengths to help you support them in overcoming their difficulties. This will build self-esteem and confidence.

More ideas

- Make up a song together about the things the child is good at. You could sing 'Matthew can work the CD player, the CD player, the CD player, Matthew can work the CD player, I saw him this afternoon' (to the tune of Here We Go Round the Mulberry Bush).

- Encourage children to be as independent as possible in your setting – getting things out, clearing up, using tools, mixing paint, making their own creations etc.

Specially for babies

- Find some simple toys with buttons to press, knobs to turn, flaps to lift. If they light up, or make music or sounds, they will be even better and more exciting.

- Let babies explore independently as much as you can, while still keeping them safe. Praise them for doing things themselves and tell their parents about it.

I can look after you!

Caring for someone else

What you need

- A baby doll in pyjamas
- Doll's clothes to fit
- A doll's pushchair or pram
- A doll's blanket
- A shopping bag or basket

What you do

1. It's a good idea to invest in some dolls with a range of clothes that fit! They will be very useful resources for all sorts of language activities and games, as well as reinforcing care of babies and younger children as children get involved in free domestic play. You could do this activity in the home corner.

2. Start with the doll or teddy in its night clothes, and ask the child to help you get the baby ready to go for a walk outside. You may suggest the baby needs a bath before you go!

3. Let the child help to collect the things you need and put some water and bubbles in the bath. Help the child to bath the baby (if they need help), talking through what they are doing and praising how carefully they are looking after it.

4. Dry and dress the baby together, still talking about what you are doing and emphasising the care the child is taking as they look after the baby. Give plenty of praise.

5. When the baby is ready, put it in the pram or pushchair while you clear up. Then take the baby out for a walk together.

Being there – playing, watching, listening, talking

- Try to resist helping too much! Talking through what you are doing together will help them. Using descriptive language and a bit of prediction will help if they are finding it difficult – 'You are holding the baby very carefully. Are you going to hold her head so she doesn't fall off your knee?' or 'You are doing this so well. Have you remembered to dry her legs? It will be easier to get the clothes on if she is dry all over.' 'Would you like me to hold the towel while you get the baby out of the bath? Babies are very slippery.' 'Don't forget to strap her in the pushchair so she doesn't fall out.'

More ideas

- Look in a mail order catalogue or on the internet for pictures of baby things and make a scrapbook.
- Cut out pictures of babies in magazines and tak about what babies need and do.
- Sing lullabies to dolls and teddies as you rock them gently and quietly.

Specially for babies

- Even young babies love baby doll play. Let them help you to bath a baby doll in lots of bubbly water. Then put the baby to bed in a blanket or cot.
- Look at books and stories about babies.

I play you play
Simple musical instruments

What you need

- A basket of simple musical instruments – shakers, rattles, bells, tambourines – at least two of each

What you do

1. Look at the music basket together, exploring all the instruments and the sounds each one makes. Talk about their names and which ones you like best.

2. Choose an instrument each and have a go at playing together. Don't worry if the timing is a bit strange!

3. Now suggest that you play 'I play, you play'. Explain that the child can play their instrument and you will copy them.

4. Let the child choose an instrument and you find the same sort.

5. When you are both ready, the child plays a short rhythm, which you copy. Try to follow them, you are aiming to build success and confidence. Praise their efforts.

6. Carry on doing this for about four repeats, then ask the child if they would like you to be the leader. If they do, repeat the same game.

7. You could ask some more children to join you, and let the first child show them what to do.

Being there – playing, watching, listening, talking

- Watch how confidently they take the lead with the instruments. Help or prompt them if they are uncertain, or demonstrate by being the leader first if that's what they want.

- Use your judgement about whether to invite more children to join the activity, the first child may find it difficult.

- If they enjoy the activity, try using music or rhythm to help them at other times.

More ideas

- Read some stories about bands, such as 'The Happy Hedgehog Band' (Candlewick Press).

- Get a copy of 'The Handy Band' by Sue Nicholls (A&C Black) – it has hundreds of ideas for music for under fives.

- Let the children play their own music by providing a basket of instruments for free play. (Outside in a tent is a good idea!)

Specially for babies

- Share simple musical instruments with babies – help them to shake, tap and rattle instruments as you hold them.

- Find some baby sized bell bracelets for wrists and ankles, or hang some bells on ribbons for babies to kick and pat with feet and hands (watch carefully so babies don't get tangled in the strings).

Snip it, and post it

Cutting and handling small things

What you need

- Paper (recycled paper is ideal)
- Round ended scissors
- A cardboard box or plastic container with a lid
- Crayons or pens

What you do

1. This activity will help children who are having difficulty with fine motor control. It is unstructured and has no 'wrong way' to do it. The snipping activity is not about cutting out, just about the skill of cutting. Make sure the scissors are sharp enough to cut paper – if they aren't, get some new ones!

2. Make a slot in the top of the box or container. It should be wide enough to slip in a bit of snipped paper but narrow enough to present some challenge to the child.

3. Cut the paper into strips about 2cm (3/4") wide.

4. Sit with the child and share this simple snipping activity, which involves snipping the strips into bits and posting the bits through the slot in the top of the box.

5. Hold your hand over theirs to help them with the snipping if they need it – however, most children can do this activity unaided.

6. You could make marks on some of the snipped bits if you want to, but the activity is usually satisfying in itself.

Being there – playing, watching, listening, talking

- Watch the child and how they use the scissors. It's not easy to spot left handers at this age, but you could start by always giving children the scissors in their right hand. If they consistently swap them to their left hand, they may be developing a preference.

- Many children love this activity and will spend long periods of time just snipping. It develops confidence, hand control and concentration. Give praise for all these.

More ideas

- Make some more different sized and shaped holes to post paper snippings through.

- Try the activity with autumn leaves, collected from your outdoor area or the park. This will give a quite different snipping sensation.

- Offer some thick needles and wool to thread the snipped pieces, adding beads or pasta tubes.

Specially for babies

- Offer different sorts of papers to babies for scrunching, tearing and squeezing. This will strengthen their hands and fingers so they are ready for more complex skills.

- Try posting screwed up paper into toy post boxes or small empty containers.

I can cook!

Simple food making

What you need

- Sliced brown bread, cut in halves (straight or diagonal)
- Soft margarine or butter
- Plates
- Jam, Marmite, honey or other spread
- Blunt ended knives (butter knives are ideal)

What you do

1. Simple food preparation is a great confidence booster, specially when you can make your own food and some to share. Try to involve those children who lack confidence in preparing snacks and picnics for the other children. They will really enjoy making this contribution to the group and you will be able to watch how their abilities are growing.

2. Making sandwiches is an activity which even very young children can do independently. They just need safe knives and soft butter, some fillings to choose from and someone to offer their sandwiches to!

3. Stay around in case they need help, but try to just talk them through any difficulties without taking over.

4. When the sandwiches are done, you may want to cut them into quarters before serving them to other children indoors or at an outdoor picnic. Make sure you give the chefs the praise they deserve and let them take the sandwiches round.

Being there – playing, watching, listening, talking

- Watch for confidence levels, hand control and ability to make choices as they select fillings.

- Give plenty of praise as they work, noticing the skills they are using and giving clear commendation such as 'That's very good spreading,' or 'Is that your favourite filling? I like jam too.' or 'You have arranged your sandwiches very carefully on the plate.'

- Make sure the chefs also help with the clearing up. This is good practice in independence too.

More ideas

- As their skills increase, try making french bread pizzas, cutting up vegetables for soup, making toast, chopping fresh vegetables to eat with yogurt dip, or making new sandwich fillings such as chopping hard-boiled egg, slicing tomatoes, making hummous or grating cheese.

Specially for babies

- Build babies' confidence with food by offering finger food whenever you can. Start early with pasta shapes, raisins or small pieces of cooked vegetables.

- Play tea parties with plastic tea sets and water, tiny sandwiches and little cheese squares. Invite a teddy or doll to join you as you snack.

Throw and catch

Building physical confidence

What you need

- A cardboard box or bucket
- Lots of rolled up pairs of socks

What you do

1. Another way to promote confidence and self-esteem is by making physical activities manageable for small hands.

2. Collect the things you need and invite the child to join you in a throwing game.

3. Share out the rolled up socks between you and ask the child where they think you should put the box or bucket. Follow their lead – they may put it miles away and have to move it, but resist the temptation to tell them before they have tried!

4. Take turns to throw the socks into the box or bucket. Don't make it a competition, just a shared activity. Talk as you play, commenting on the way the child is throwing, asking them if they want to move the box nearer or further away, praising their successes and sympathising when they miss.

5. When you have used up all the socks, tip them all out and play again, but this time, put the box or bucket on its side.

Being there – playing, watching, listening, talking

- Watch for the development of a preferred hand for throwing.

- Try to be a supportive partner, not an aggressive competitor! Your role is to support and extend confidence and competence.

- Be tactful when making suggestions about throwing style or where to put the box or bucket.

- If the child finds things difficult in the future, remind them of their successes in this game and other activities from this book. Talk openly about how some things are easier to do than others, and that everyone has things they are good at.

More ideas

- Try fishing plastic balls out of a bowl of water with tweezers or tongs.

- Put the pairs of socks in some water, and then use them to throw against a wall for 'Splat Shot', or drop them from the climbing frame into a bucket or a chalk circle on the ground.

Specially for babies

- Play passing games and giving games, where the child can fetch things from a basket and give them to you.

- Dropping objects into a box or bowl gives practice with letting go – this is a skill in itself.

With love from me to you

Messages, letters and cards

What you need

- Paper and card of different shapes, sizes and colours

- Envelopes

- Scissors, sticky tape and glue sticks

- Magazines and catalogues

- Pencils, crayons, pens

What you do

1. Sending messages, letters, pictures and cards is a great way to build confidence and approach others.

2. You could offer this activity to the whole group and sit with the less confident child as they work.

3. Look through the things that are available – less confident children often find it difficult to start an activity and this is why they tend to flit from one to another or sit without doing anything.

4. Don't be in too much of a hurry to start. Take time to talk about who they want to send a message to, what sort of things that person likes, which of the resources they are going to use.

5. Once they are getting started, just watch what happens, offering help if they need it, but not taking over. Reflect back what they are doing in a quiet 'running commentary' as they work, praising what they are doing and making gentle suggestions if they seem to get stuck.

Being there – playing, watching, listening, talking

- Just being there is really important to less confident children, and is often all they need – a nod, smile or a few words are often all it needs to keep them going and concentrating.

- Observe and note creative ideas, strengths and skills. This is often a good opportunity to do a long observation of one or two children as you give support and guidance or just your presence.

- Sometimes make something too, but be careful that children don't just try to make the same as you. You may need to use your judgement about joining in or standing back.

More ideas

- Try to offer free choice and independence to all the children as you make cards, letters and messages. Have a post box. Don't all make the same Mother's Day or Christmas cards. Provide a wide range of materials and be there to discuss with them what they would like to make. This will give all the children more confidence.

Specially for babies

- Offer babies stickers and other self-adhesive objects to stick on paper or in little books. Let them wrap things in paper for gifts, explore envelopes, wrapping paper and gift bags. Praise their efforts at sticking, wrapping, folding and scrunching paper and receive gifts gracefully!

How do you feel?

Exploring feelings

What you need

- Paper plates
- Short garden sticks or straws
- Magazines
- Scissors and glue sticks

What you do

1. This simple mask/puppet making activity is easy and good fun. You may want to find some of the pictures in advance, so you have a wide range of expressions. Adverts, and 'Mother and Toddler' magazines will give you lots of faces of babies and children.

2. Start by looking at the magazines together, looking particularly at faces and expressions. Tear some of these pages out of the magazines, choosing pictures that are big enough to see the expressions well. Add your previously prepared ones if you need them.

3. When you have a good collection of different faces, spread them out on the table or floor and talk about each, discussing the names of the expressions – happy, sad, cross, friendly, scared etc.

4. Now help the child to cut out the faces and stick them on the paper plates. Attach a stick to each and your face masks are ready to use

5. Play with the child, putting masks in front of your faces and saying – 'How do I feel now?' or 'I'm going to get really cross now!'. Reading expressions is an important skill for all children, less confident ones may need more practice.

Being there – playing, watching, listening, talking

- Note whether the child can recognise expressions in photos. Some less confident children are not very good at reading expressions and may need more help with recognising the features of faces in different photos.

- Watch them as they play at putting on the expressions. Can they choose a face for the feeling? Can they copy the expression with their own face? Can they recognise which face you are making?

More ideas

- Use the masks in group time to make up stories.
- Use them at Circle time or group times. Children can choose one to describe how they are feeling.
- Look for more photos to add to your collection, or ask the older children to draw some with felt pens or crayons.

Specially for babies

- Use the faces with babies, but be careful not to frighten them!
- Make some simple black and white 'smiling face' puppets using paper plates and black felt pens. Young babies respond well to black and white patterns and faces. Use these faces to attract their attention and help them with tracking from one side to another.

69

Advice

Some tips for practitioners:

- Watch for the triggers – they may be different for different children.

- Note which activities seem particularly stressful to the child – this is often a clue, particularly if it's the same thing every time – using scissors, going outside, group times, making things.

- Make an effort to find out the things the child can do – you will need to know as part of your plan.

- React calmly, sit with the child and see if you can help – if not, remove the child from the activity or the activity from the child by getting them involved in something they do enjoy and can do.

Some tips to share with parents:

Parents can help their child to deal with lack of confidence by:

- showing understanding, and trying not to be impatient

- acknowledging the child's feelings, and perhaps remembering times when they were less confident

- acknowledging the child's feelings by saying, 'I know you think you can't do this, and don't want to try, but I will help you' etc.

- keeping their expectations reasonable

- trying not to show disappointment or frustration when their child says 'I can't'

- praising their child for the things they do with confidence, even if they seem very simple

- noticing any successes and praising these appropriately

- remembering how difficult it was to do new things when they were children

- making time at the end of every day to talk about the day gives the child the chance to tell them the things they have enjoyed and done well

- keeping in mind that, with their parents' help and support, most children will regain their sense of self-esteem and a 'have a go' attitude.

Try to be a good role model. Children look to the most important people in their life and try to imitate their behaviour.

Who's This?

Adjusting to a new role

Contents

Introduction

Having a new baby at home is a perfectly natural part of everyday life, and many children adapt to their new role in the family with confidence and ease, but for some children, the new arrival can cause strong feelings, mixed emotions and much confusion. How children understand and express their emotions and adapt to their new life depends on many factors including their:

- developmental stage
- position in their family and the attention they are used to
- personality and communication skills
- relationship with key people in their life
- opportunity to make choices
- ability to express their feelings

and:

- how much disruption there is to routine
- the length of time they are separated from their parents.

Older children need time to adjust when the new baby brother or sister is brought home. The amount of attention they feel they are losing and what else is happening in the child's life will also affect their feelings and responses.

The age and particularly the developmental stage of the child is very important. At around twelve months, a child may sense that his/her mother is different but may not attribute that change to the new baby.

At around two years of age, the child's world will still revolve entirely around their parents or carers and their emotional well-being will be dependent on attachment to them and the consistency with which they respond to needs. By around three years of age, the child's seemingly growing independence and egocentricity, and the increasing importance of friends may enable the child to more readily accept a new sibling.

But every child and every family is different and a child may seem to be coping well with this fundamental change in their lives, but days or even weeks later may experience a range of strong emotions.

Topic 5: Introduction

What you might see and what the child might be feeling

Every child and every set of circumstances is unique, but young children are far more likely to show us how they are feeling long before they are able to understand what they are feeling or tell us in words.

Any change in mood or behaviour may be a child's response to a new situation, but you might see:

- regression to much younger behaviour, such as wanting to be fed, or toilet training accidents

- attention seeking behaviour

- separation anxiety

- waking at night

- difficulty with friendships and sharing

- becoming unusually quiet or withdrawn.

A child might be feeling any or all of these:

Practitioners need to be mindful of any changes in behaviour, observe the child carefully and discuss the child's needs with the parent.

A new baby map

What do new babies really like?

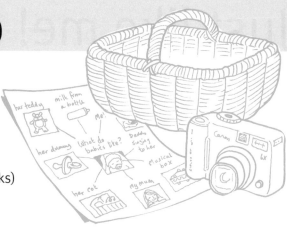

What you need

- 'Peepo' by Janet and Allan Ahlberg (Viking Children's Books)
- Baby equipment catalogues and brochures
- A big sheet of paper, pens, glue, scissors
- Camera and printer
- Small basket

What you do

1. Share 'Peepo' together. Talk about what new babies need, such as love, warmth, milk, smiles, play. Agree to make a big map of what babies need.

2. Help the child to find and cut out pictures of babies in the catalogues and magazines. Stick these in the centre of their map. In one corner of the map, draw a picture of a baby rattle, and in other parts of the map, draw a face, a baby bath, a food bowl, a cot, a baby blanket. Just simple line drawings will be fine.

3. Now help the child to gather toys, objects and pictures of things that babies need, such as a baby blanket, bottle, baby clothes etc. You could arrange to visit the baby room in your setting. Put these in the basket, take photos of each and print them for the map.

4. Make the map personal by asking parents for photos of the family to add to the child's map. It is important for the child to know that the new baby needs them too.

5. Display the map and the objects in the basket carefully. Don't forget to add a photo of the child and the new baby once it has arrived.

Being there – playing, watching, listening, talking

- Take your time sharing the story book. Give the child plenty of opportunities to study the pictures and think about their new baby without having to talk.

- Reassure the child that the love and attention the new baby needs is just the same sort of love and attention they need.

- Observe body language carefully. The child may be telling you far more non-verbally than they are saying in words.

More ideas

- Look through baby equipment and toy catalogues together and talk about the sorts of soft toys the child likes and what they had as a baby? What do they like about their comfort toy?

- Visit a baby clinic together and watch the babies being weighed and measured and dressed.

Specially for babies

- Make extra time for one-to-one play, singing, dancing and hugging. They may not understand that a new baby is coming, but they may be unsettled by changes to routine at home.

- Look at simple photo books together, naming everyday objects related to homes, families and babies.

Just like me!

Remembering when I was a baby

What you need

- Baby photos of the child
- Selection of baby toys, baby books and baby clothes
- Safety mirror
- Card, sticky tape, coloured pens, collage materials

What you do

1. Look through the baby photos together, and talk about how the child looked when they were a baby.

2. Encourage the child to think about similarities and differences between now and then. Use the mirror to help as you talk about the child's hair now and as a baby, their eye colour and so on.

3. Talk together about the sorts of things the child liked to do as a baby. What were their favourite baby toys? What baby clothes did they have? Have they still got some of these?

4. Make a photo frame for a picture of the child with the new baby when it has arrived. For lots of ideas for simple photo frames try www.activityvillage.co.uk. Keep it simple, the most important part of this activity is taking time to be an effective listener for the child.

Being there – playing, watching, listening, talking

- Make sure that the staff team understands that you need uninterrupted time with the child.

- Sit alongside the child and be comfortable with silence. They may need lots of time to respond.

- If the child is struggling to explain their feelings about their new baby, why not share a sheet of paper at the easel and paint families together. Quietly working alongside the child is often all it takes to give them the confidence to express their feelings in words, painting or play.

More ideas

- Use a stethoscope to listen to children's heart beats. Play at listening to a doll's heart beat.

- Make a 'Baby Can' picture. Talk about all the things that babies can do, such as look, listen, sleep, cry, gurgle, suck and so on. As each idea comes, draw a little baby symbol showing the baby doing just that.

- Set up a small obstacle course with cushions, hoops and so on. Complete the course by rolling, crawling or shuffling like a baby.

Specially for babies

- Sing lullaby songs with the child. Encourage them to hold a baby doll as you rock together. Sing traditional rhymes such as 'Rock a Bye Baby' or 'Lavender's Blue Dilly Dilly'. Go to www.babycentre. co.uk/baby/sleep/lullaby for more.

Games babies play

Games for my new baby

What you need

- Paint and paper for making hand prints
- Scissors and glue
- Thin card to make a mini booklet
- Google images of babies playing finger and toe games

What you do

1. Explain that babies love to have people play with their fingers and toes. Talk about the sorts of gentle blowing, kissing and tickle games they could play with the new baby.

2. Make a small book together, decorated with the child's hand prints. Try out and add these games for fingers and toes to the book.

3. Ask the child to suggest their own ideas, favourite finger rhymes and so on. Work together, helping the child to find and draw pictures to illustrate each page.

Tickle in Turn
Gently stroke the back of the baby's hand and then up and down each finger in turn, sing:

'Tiny fingers, tiny fingers, tickle and kiss, tickle and kiss, tiny fingers, tiny fingers, all in mine.'

Kiss and Count
Kiss and count each finger in turn:

'One little finger, kiss,

two little fingers, kiss kiss,

three little fingers, kiss, kiss, kiss.'

Blow Wind Blow
Sing 'Blow wind blow' and then blow a tiny puff of air onto each finger and then a longer gentle blow into the palm of the hand, play again on the other hand or maybe with feet and toes.

Being there – playing, watching, listening, talking

- When you see the child with the new baby at the beginning of the day, be sure to greet the child first and talk with them for a few moments and then include them in your smiling and saying hello to the baby. Be sure to finish any exchange with the focus on the child, not the baby.

- Make sure the child knows it is fine to still enjoy all these games – they are not just for babies.

- Take your time and offer lots of specific praise and encouragement.

More ideas

- Create a new version of finger and toe play games for the child to share with the new baby – 'This little baby went to sleep, this little baby had a bath', and so on.

- Practise massaging tiny amounts of baby oil into each others' hands. It is a lovely, relaxing activity and something the child may be able to help the parents do for the baby.

Specially for babies

- Play 'Round and Round the Garden like a Teddy Bear' and other early finger plays and tickle games. Ask the child to do the actions to you as you sing the rhyme again.

- Look at a range of baby toys together, either in the early years setting or in picture books. Talk about the sorts of toys the baby might like to play with – rattles to listen to, mobiles to look at, soft toys to feel.

In the picture

A special photo frame

What you need

- Craft foam sheets
- Scissors and glue
- Photos of the family
- Magnet strips

What you do

1. Help the child to make a simple magnet photo frame using a sheet of craft foam. Cut the foam into a shape, using a template if you need one. You can find templates by looking on Google, or visiting websites for craft activities.

2. Fix the magnet strips to the back of the frame.

3. Look at the family photos together and talk about the people in them. You may want to scan or photocopy the photos if the child is likely to be upset by cutting up the originals. Or you could take some photos of the child specially for this activity.

4. Now help the child to cut out faces from the family photos and stick them round the frame to decorate it.

5. Talk together about what makes a family special, like love, caring, doing things together, and so on.

6. Encourage the child to talk about what things might change and what things will stay the same about their family with the new baby.

Being there – playing, watching, listening, talking

- Encourage the child to talk about their relationships with all the family, including their grandparents. The child's extended family can be hugely important in helping the child develop self-esteem and trust.

- Try and let the child take the lead. The finished frame needs to be all their own work, so their achievement can be recognized and kept at home in a special place.

More ideas

- Play together, sorting and washing baby clothes. Use this as an opportunity for the child to talk to you about how they are feeling.
- Put lots of baby accessories in the home corner, together with parenting magazines and baby equipment catalogues.

Specially for babies

- Put some baby objects in a 'feely box' and play a guessing game. Name and talk about how a tiny baby might need each object – a nappy, bottle, baby brush etc.
- Stick a photo of the child on an old CD. Cover the other side with white paper and then encourage the child to make marks on the paper with black pens. Thread ribbon through the CD to make a mobile for the new baby.

Give me the moon papa

Stories of loving families

What you need

- Baby doll
- Small blanket for the child
- Eric Carle's book 'Papa, Please Get the Moon for Me' (Simon & Schuster), or a book from the resources section

What you do

1. Snuggle up together with the blanket wrapped around the child, and the child looking after the baby doll.

2. Look at the pictures in the book together. The main character is a small child and the theme is one of unconditional love.

3. Take your time reading the story and looking at the pictures together.

4. Encourage the child to talk about the emotions characters might be feeling. Help them to find the right words to describe the feelings.

5. Let them talk about their parents and what they do for them.

6. Try to make some quiet time for every child – ideally every day. Focus on your key group of children.

Being there – playing, watching, listening, talking

- Observe carefully how the child holds and handles the doll during the story.

- Encourage the child to turn the pages when they are ready. Let them go back to favourite parts they want to hear again.

- Listen to the language they use to talk about feelings.

More ideas

- Extend the activity by reading together 'Mama Do You Love Me?' by Barbara Joose (Chronicle Books). This is a tale of a young Inuit child testing the love of her mother as she seeks more independence. 'Clever Daddy' by Maddie Stewart (Walker Books) is a lovely book to share as a reminder of the fun dads can have with babies and very young children.

Specially for babies

- Look for simple photo books of everyday objects for babies, such as a brush, nappy, bottle, rattle, blanket and so on.

- Sit an older baby on your knee and give them a baby doll to hold. Play gentle tickle and finger games, first with the baby, then with the baby doll. Encourage the baby to try the game on the baby doll.

Big sister big brother

Design a t-shirt

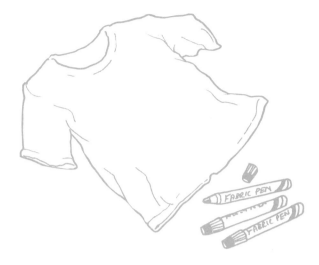

What you need

- Washed and ironed small plain white t-shirt
- Fabric pens
- Sheet of card
- Mirror
- Photograph of the child as a baby

What you do

1. Look together at the photograph of the child as a baby. Talk about how they have grown.

2. Look in the mirror and talk about how they look now compared to how they looked as a baby.

3. Wonder aloud how the new baby will look when they are three or four years old? What does the big brother or sister think?

4. Be alongside the child as they use fabric pens to draw a picture of themselves on the t-shirt. You may need to hold the t-shirt flat and firm for them. Encourage them to keep looking back at the mirror to check their features and to add more detail to their drawing.

5. Help them to add their name. Do they want to add pictures of anyone else in their family? Do they want to add a big sister/brother label?

6. Wash and iron according to the instructions to fix the colour to the fabric.

Being there – playing, watching, listening, talking

- Give the child time to develop their ideas.
- Ask open questions that help them think about their role as big brother or big sister and how this will change over time.
- Reassure children that how we feel often changes from day to day or over time. Talk about how they can let you and their parents know how they are feeling.

More ideas

- Cut a small piece of fleece and help the child to use fabric pens to make a mini blanket for the new baby.
- Make a family flag, with names and drawings of the family.
- Use the child's photo to make a special welcome baby sister/baby brother card.
- Use fabric glue and the pens to make a simple finger puppet for play with the new baby.

Specially for babies

- Provide lots of baby dolls, baby blankets and feeding bottles for simple pretend play.
- Try some finger painting with baby lotion. It has a lovely texture on a plastic tray. While you paint talk about how the older baby was looked after when they were very tiny.

Bath time fun

Bath your own baby

What you need

- Baby bath
- Tiny quantities of baby shampoo, baby
- Toothbrush, towel
- Baby talcum powder
- Nappy and baby clothes
- Baby doll

What you do

1. Help the child to fill the bath with warm water. Add some baby bubble bath.

2. Play alongside the child as they bath the baby doll. You could even have a baby doll of your own to share the bath.

3. Provide a simple commentary describing what you are doing together.

4. Show the child little games the baby might enjoy with the water, such as trickling water onto the doll's toes, helping the baby to pat the water with open hands to make little splashes, or swishing up bubbles.

5. Talk to the child about what they like to do at bath time. Do they like to play with bath toys? Use bath crayons? Have bubbles? Slide on the wet bath? Talk about how important all the cuddles and hugs are as they are wrapped in the warm towel to dry.

6. Help the child to dry and dress the baby doll. Sing some baby songs to the baby and put them snugly to bed.

Being there – playing, watching, listening, talking

- Listen to the language the child uses to describe what they are doing and report on what happens at bath time at home.

- Think about their helping role and try to make it as much fun as possible. The child may want some responsibility but they also need to feel an important part of the fun.

- Praise the child for their gentleness. Talk about how the baby might feel.

More ideas

- With a small sponge each, play alongside the child singing 'This is the way we wash the toes, wash the toes, wash the toes etc'.

- Add a baby bath support.

- Give the child a flannel to protect the baby doll's eyes while you shampoo the baby's hair.

- Add some plastic ducks and sing 'Five Little Ducks'.

Specially for babies

- Give an older baby a small baby doll and a small wet flannel to wash the baby. Help them to dry the baby.

- Dress a baby doll together. Give them plenty of choices. Can they help pull clothes on? or perhaps hold the baby doll's hand to help it through the sleeve?

My family book

A book about us

What you need

- Sheet of A4 paper
- Pens
- Scissors
- Collage materials

What you do

1. Cut a sheet of A4 paper in half lengthways and tape the two pieces together along the short edges to make one very long sheet.

2. Fold the edge in by about 7cm, turn the paper over and fold again, as if you were making a paper fan. Continue until you have a small concertina book.

3. Ask the child to draw a picture of themself on the front page of the book. Now complete the pages together, with pictures of each family member, special friends and so on. Add favourite colours, birthday cakes with candles to show how old the children are and anything else the child suggests.

4. Leave a page for the new baby if it hasn't arrived yet!

5. Encourage the child to show the booklet to other staff and their parents, talking about their family and friends.

6. Reassure the child how lucky they are to have so many people who love and care for them.

Being there – playing, watching, listening, talking

- Give the child plenty of time to talk about each member of their family. Focus on what they enjoy doing together.

- Listen to the child talking about the new baby and their relationship with him/her.

- Make sure the child spends plenty of time completing their own page, with pictures of what they like, what they enjoy doing, what they want to do when they are older and so on.

More ideas

- Try some simple weaving together of ribbons, wool and string through netting. Tape pictures of the things the family like doing to the woven background. Weaving together is very relaxing and will give you plenty of time to listen to the child. Encourage them to talk about how things change when families grow.

Specially for babies

- Make a simple photo book for the child with their cup on one side of the page, and the new baby's bottle on the other. On the next page have a picture of their bed or cot and another picture of the new baby's cot or bed and so on. Use catalogues or magazines for pictures.

I'd rather have an iguana!

A talk and turn-taking game

What you need

- 'Barfburger Baby, I Was Here First', by Paula Danziger (Puffin Books) or a book from the resources section

- Basket of small toys – teddy bear, dinosaur, tiger, and so on

- Two floor cushions

What you do

1. Share the book with the child. Ask open questions and listen carefully to what they think the little boy is feeling. Reassure the child that the boy's feelings were very real and that perhaps it took quite a long time for the boy to always feel pleased about the new baby. Reassure the child that lots of big brothers and sisters feel like that, but love always grows, sometimes straight away and sometimes more slowly and that's okay.

2. Tell the child you know a funny game the boy could have played.

3. Sit opposite each other on the floor cushions with the basket of small toys.

4. Choose one of the toys from the basket, maybe a dinosaur, and say or sing:

   'I have a new baby, maybe that's cool,

   maybe it's not,

   maybe I'd rather have .....a dinosaur'.

   Hand the basket to the child to choose a toy and sing again.

   'I have a new baby, maybe that's cool,

   maybe it's not,

   maybe I'd rather have .....a bear'.

   Play on, taking turns. Make it fun and light hearted.

Being there – playing, watching, listening, talking

- Bring another child into the game if the child feels anxious about admitting feelings of frustration about their baby.

- Use simple words to describe feelings. Talk about the different ways people can tell how they are feeling.

- Watch the child's body language carefully. It may be a clue to how the child is really feeling.

More ideas

- For more light hearted discussion, share 'Avocado Baby' by John Burningham (Red Fox).

- Help the child to find lots of clip art images, simply Google 'clipart babies'. Print and make a collage or number line of babies. This will provide lots of opportunities to share a gentle laugh about babies and their antics.

Specially for babies

- Show an older baby how to play peek-a-boo with a hat or cloth with younger babies.

- Find some sunglasses with plastic frames. Play a silly turn-taking imitating actions game.

- Find some baby faces board books to share. See the Resources section for a list.

Special times

Toys and games for busy times

What you need

- Shoe box or similar
- Toy catalogue
- Scissors and glue
- Large sheets of coloured paper
- Paint in shallow tray for hand prints

What you do

1. Put some paint in shallow trays and help the child to make hand prints all over the large sheet of paper. While the child is doing the hand prints talk about how there will be times when mummy will be busy feeding the new baby, and that it's a good idea to make a special box to fill with toys so they can play next to mummy when she is feeding the baby.

2. When the paint is dry, help the child to cover the box with the hand printed paper.

3. Choose pictures of favourite toys from the catalogue and paste onto the outside of the box.

4. Help the child to add their name.

5. Make a note for the parents, asking them to take a few minutes to help the child fill the box with some of their favourite small toys and books.

6. Keep the box ready for when mum is feeding the baby.

Being there – playing, watching, listening, talking

- Talk to the child about how much new babies need to sleep and explain that there may be some times when mummy is busy with the baby, but there will also be lots of time the baby is asleep and then parents will have more time for them.

- Listen carefully to the child to find out how much they already know about tiny babies.

- Enjoy this activity together, making it really special. Ask the child what they have decided to put in their box.

More ideas

- Print some simple colouring and puzzle pages from the internet for the child to add to their box.

- Suggest putting a box of dressing up clothes next to baby at feeding time.

- Make sure that details of the local toy library and book lending library are on the parents' notice board in the setting.

Specially for babies

- Put some baby board books in a small bag for the parent.

- Suggest a basket of big socks, hats and gloves as a great way of keeping older babies occupied whilst the parent is busy feeding the new baby.

Send that baby back!

A hug-me game and scrap book

What you need

- Simple scrap book – a home-made one is fine
- Digital camera

What you do

1. This game works well when a child is feeling left out and cross!

2. Play a game of traffic lights with the child and a friend, calling 'red' (jump), 'orange' (hug), 'green' (walk)! Use lots of energy with this fun running and chasing game. The children take turns to be the caller. When 'orange' is called, the caller has to try and catch the runner for a hug!

3. Lots of exercise, and the smiles of chasing and catching for a hug will help everyone feel good.

4. Ask another child to take some photos of the game. Print the photos and paste them into the scrap book.

5. Take photographs of the child with their friends doing favourite activities.

6. Help the child to add lots of smiley faces or stickers to the pages.

7. Write out the words of their favourite songs and rhymes so that other people looking at the scrap book can share the child's pride and pleasure.

Being there – playing, watching, listening, talking

- Look at the range of books in the Resources section. Choose an appropriate book to share with the child, reassuring the child that everyone can feel a bit cross about the baby, or perhaps jealous.

- Jealousy is a difficult concept for children and you might need to suggest lots of examples for them to be able to understand and use the word appropriately.

- Watch carefully to see if the child can sustain their happy mood after the game. How are their friendships being affected by their anxiety about the new baby?

More ideas

- Talk about baby noises. See how many you can name together. Talk about how each sound makes you feel.

- Find lots of pictures of babies and create a giant montage of baby pictures. As you do this together focus on what each baby's face is doing and how the baby might be feeling.

Specially for babies

- Sing Heads, Shoulders, Knees and Toes with older babies, touching each body part on the child as you sing. Help them to touch the new baby's head, shoulders, knees and toes as you sing the rhyme to both of them.

- Encourage the older baby to clap as you sing rhymes.

Welcome to the world

Make a WELCOME banner

What you need

- Lengths of ribbon
- Triangles of coloured paper
- Sticky tape
- Old CDs
- Paper and pens

What you do

1. Talk about what you are going to do – explain what a banner is and maybe look at some pictures on Google Images.

2. Let the child help you to collect all the things you need. Help the child to make some simple bunting by taping triangles of paper to a long length of ribbon.

3. Encourage the child to draw pictures and find photos to stick to the old CDs to show the new baby and visitors when they arrive home.

4. Thread shorter lengths of ribbon through the old CDs and fix to them the bunting string.

5. Talk about the new baby coming home and having visitors. Talk about what they might be able to do, such as showing visitors the new baby cards or singing to the baby.

Being there – playing, watching, listening, talking

- Perhaps the time is right for you to make a simple 'Congratulations on becoming a big brother/sister' card for the child themselves! Include the child's favourite rhyme inside so that parents can help the child sing the rhyme to the new baby.

- Try and make extra time to be with the child. Listen carefully to them and offer extra reassurance and attention.

- Always greet the child before the new baby and finish any conversation with the parent, child and new baby with specific praise for the child that does not in any way refer to the baby.

More ideas

- Stick the child's photograph in the centre of an A4 sheet of coloured card and add lots of star stickers all around it, with notes praising what the child has done well each day. Add more notes each day and ask the parents to display it with the new baby cards.

Specially for babies

- Make sure there is a small hair brush, bottle, a dolls push chair etc. available for the beginnings of simple pretend play.

- Everyone at home and in the early years setting needs to make extra one-to-one time for the older baby with a new sibling. Trying to keep routines the same will help.

Advice

Some tips for practitioners:

There is much you can do to help young children cope with feelings that emerge around the birth of a new baby. You can:

- provide opportunities for the child to express their emotions, and offer them the right words and actions to do so

- acknowledge their feelings and reassure them

- encourage children to talk about the new baby and how they feel

- provide an understanding and supportive environment

- use books and stories to help children understand their emotions

- find ways for the child to look positively at the changes

- developing quiet places to feel secure and comfortable

- be an effective listener and observer, responding to their needs

- encourage understanding in other children and staff.

Practitioners need to be mindful of any changes in behaviour, observe the child carefully and discuss the child's needs with the parent. When the parent brings the new baby to your setting with the older child:

- Greet the older child first – get down to their eye level.

- Invite the older child to introduce the new baby to the other children.

- Give positive and specific praise to the child.

- Enjoy and take time with the child and the new baby.

- Share the older child's choice of tickle game with the baby.

- Finish by talking to the parent, praising the child and saying goodbye first to the parent and new baby, and then to the child.

Some tips to share with parents

Parents can help their child to adjust to the new baby by:

- keeping the older child's routines and activities the same, as far as possible

- sharing books about new babies and growing up

- planning the day so bath and bedtime routines are unhurried

- organising suitable play activities for times when the parent is busy feeding the baby

- inviting the older child to help, without being insistent

- offering choices, such as which socks should baby wear today, which flannel should to use etc.

- making special one to one time with favourite games, songs and books

- making a point of greeting the older child with enthusiasm

- encouraging the older child to express their feelings. If they express negative feelings about the baby, parents should take care to hide their own inevitable feelings of shock, hurt and disappointment, acknowledge the child's feelings are real, and avoid the temptation to tell them they will feel better soon

- prepare visitors, and make sure they include the older child when they come to meet the new baby.

And a final tip:

Remember that siblings may appear calm and confident and adjusted to the new baby, but a few months later, when the baby is engaging and playful and may be mobile and getting into the older child's toys and games, hurt feelings may reappear.

Where Am I Going?

Dealing with change

Contents

Introduction

For many very young children moving house is an unwelcome upheaval, but their fundamental sense of security remains focused on the people most familiar to them. However, for some children, their circumstances can make moving house distressing.

Misunderstanding the concept of moving house is not uncommon in children and can create all sorts of anxieties. For children whose life is constantly changing, with new people and unpredictable circumstances, self confidence and self-esteem can also be dented.

Every baby and young child encounters change in their lives. How they cope with, understand and respond to the challenges of that change will depend on many factors unique to them, which will include their:

- developmental stage

- relationship with key people in their life

- sense of security

- self confidence and self-esteem

- personality

- communication skills

- opportunity to make choices

- ability to express their feelings.

What you might see and what the child might be feeling

Every child and every set of circumstances is unique, but young children are far more likely to show us how they are feeling long before they are able to understand what they are feeling or tell.

Any change in mood or behaviour may be a child's response to an impending move, but you might see:

- attentive children becoming inattentive

- thumb sucking or clingy behaviour

- relapses in toilet training

- tearfulness or anger

- anxiety on saying goodbye to parent or carer;

- unexplained tummy aches and headaches

- changes in behaviour such as irritability or unusual shyness

- pretending to be a much younger child.

A child might be feeling any or all of these:

Practitioners should be mindful of any changes in a child's behaviour, observe the child carefully and discuss the child's needs together, taking note of what others in the team have observed or heard.

Teddy's moving day

Home corner big box play

What you need

- Photograph or picture book illustration of moving house
- Cups, plates, spoons
- Small books, games
- Boxes, wrapping paper
- Small trolley or barrow
- Teddy

What you do

1. Hug teddy and look at the pictures together. Invite the child to help you get Teddy ready to move house.

2. Play alongside the child, wrapping and packing into the boxes. Let the child take the lead and ask open questions to prompt.

3. Build empathy by imitating the child's actions and wonder aloud how Teddy might be feeling about moving.

4. Gently describe some of the feelings Teddy might be experiencing. Reassure the child that everyone feels a bit anxious when moving.

5. Try to help the child find the right words to describe their feelings, (excited, cross, worried, scared, confused) and acknowledge any symptoms of these feelings, such as 'When I'm worried sometimes I get a funny feeling in my tummy' or 'When I'm cross I feel all hot and don't know what I want to do'.

6. Move the boxes in the trolley to the home corner and finish by hugging Teddy.

7. Leave the activity for other children to join in the play or for the child to return to later.

Being there – playing, watching, listening, talking

- Take your time and let the child approach the activity slowly.
- Mention your own memories of moving and how you felt.
- Watch the child's body language and non verbal signals, which may well tell you more about how they are feeling than they are able to with words.

More ideas

- Set up a simple dolls' house and play at moving house with small world play people.
- Try some moving day outdoor play with big cardboard boxes, marker pens to label the boxes and some trolleys.
- Make a collage of moving day pictures (try Google Images and the websites and brochures of removal companies listed in the resources section.

Specially for babies

- Reassure parents that babies' sense of security is focused on the familiar people in their lives, rather than a place.
- Wrap a teddy in a blanket and gently rock Teddy and the baby together. Take them to the home corner and put Teddy to bed, saying 'Night night Ted'.
- Make a family photo book.

Wrapping up, keeping safe

Keeping things safe

What you need

- Newspaper
- Wrapping paper
- Sticky tape
- GIft bags
- Scissors
- Cartons

What you do

1. Take time to explore the papers, strings, tape and boxes you have collected.

2. Talk about wrapping things up to keep them safe and stop them breaking.

3. Take a walk round the setting and collect a few things to wrap up. You could look for favourite toys or books, puzzles etc. Collect lots of different shapes and sizes.

4. Use the materials to wrap up some of the toys and other equipment, and put them in a carton. Talk about how they fit in, whether they move about inside the box and whether they are safe in there.

5. Try wrapping up some difficult shapes such as a ball or a toy phone.

6. When they have had enough, enjoy unwrapping all the things to check if they are still alright.

Being there – playing, watching, listening, talking

- Encourage them to be as independent as possible in using tape and scissors, only helping if asked. Use positive talk to encourage them.

- Work alongside, wrapping too, and talking about what you are doing, 'This will keep my ...... safe, so it won't break. I'll be able to unpack it when we get there. The removal men will carry it carefully in their van.'

- Talk and listen to conversations about special things and keeping them safe.

More ideas

- Explore some bubble wrap for a bit of fun and laughter!

- Take the wrapped objects outside in a truck or basket and see if they stay safe.

Specially for babies

- Babies will love exploring the paper and other wrappings.

- Talk with parents about doing some of the packing where babies can see them and hear them talk about keeping the things safe for the new house.

My special box

A special collection

What you need

- Digital camera and printer
- PVA glue
- Scissors
- Strong cardboard box
- Magazines and catalogues from removal companies

What you do

1. Look through the pictures together. Talk about the process of packing boxes, labelling and putting them on a van. Talk about the van arriving at their new home, unloading and unpacking.

2. Tell the child that you want to help them make and label a special box for their most precious toys. Talk about the sorts of things you might put in your box and ask what they might like to put in their special box.

3. Cut out pictures and decorate the box. Help the child to put a name on the box.

4. Use the camera to take photographs of the child's favourite toys. Ask parents to help with this by bringing in toys to be photographed.

5. Add a picture of the child. Be sure to include a photo of the child's main comfort toy or blanket.

6. Encourage the child to keep their favourite soft toys and other toys in the box.

7. Explain that sometimes things do get lost but, if all their favourite things go in this special box then everyone will know that the box needs special care.

Being there – playing, watching, listening, talking

- Help the child to take the lead in decorating the box. Make it really special – just for them.

- Listen to them talking about moving and prompt them to think and talk about what will happen when they have moved. Talk about their new home, focusing on similarities with their home now.

- If they are feeling really cross about the move, give them a second cardboard box spnd something safe to bash it with!

More ideas

- Use thin card and a paper punch to make simple parcel tags. Colour and mark the tags to make labels for the child's most precious possessions.

- Paint together at the easel. Talk about feelings.

Specially for babies

- Keep routines within the setting as clear as possible. Ensure the baby's key worker greets them each morning.

- If the baby is moving to a new setting, make a passport with photos and details of their time with you, likes, dislikes, routines, rhymes, songs and picture books.

My room and my bed

Missing old things and welcoming new

What you need

- Safe bedside light
- Dolls' or baby bedclothes
- Catalogues
- Soft toys
- Shoe boxes

What you do

1. Collect toy bedclothes and a soft toy each, and talk about bedtime.

2. As you talk, begin to make a bed for your toy, and encourage the child to do so with their toy.

3. Talk about bedclothes, pillows and what sort you like, asking them what their bed is like – the pattern on their bedspread or duvet, their wallpaper, light, toys and books. Let them tell you about their bedtime routine, favourite bedtime toy or toys and if they have these toys in bed with them. Reassure them that their bed will still be there in the new house.

4. Find some catalogues and look for pictures of bedding and other bedroom objects that they know and like. Cut some of these out to make a picture of their room.

Being there – playing, watching, listening, talking

- Make sure you talk to parents so you don't make promises that can't be kept. Find out what the new situation is going to be!

- Listen to the child and note any signs of anxiety about leaving their bedroom, and reassure them that their bed and their toys will be there to meet them in their new house.

More ideas

- Make a bedroom in a pop-up tent or shelter.
- Offer children sleeping bags for role play indoors and outside.
- Find some torches and have fun in a tent.

Specially for babies

- Remember that sense of smell is the most evocative of all senses. The smell of pillows, sheets and duvets is very special to babies, so this is NOT the time for a new mattress, pillow or duvet cover! You may even suggest to parents that they don't wash the baby's bed linen the night before they move.

Old friends, new friends

All my friends in a row

What you need

- Plain paper strip, about 12cm by 60cm
- Marker pen
- Small scissors
- Pens and crayons

What you do

1. Together fold the strip of paper accordion style so each panel is about 6cm wide.

2. Help the child to draw a simple outline of a child on the front panel, making sure that parts of the body (hands and feet) or clothing (jeans or skirts) touch the sides of the panel. (This is where the dolls hands and feet join.)

3. Cut around the outline but don't cut along the folds where the body parts or clothes touch the edge of the panel.

4. Unfold the chain of dolls and decorate them with pens or crayons.

5. Encourage the child to make some dolls of current friends, adding names.

6. Help them to imagine new friends they might make in their new setting or home and to decorate some of the paper dolls as their new friends.

7. Make the paper doll chain into a circle including the old and new friends.

    See the resources section for websites where you can get paperdoll templates.

Being there – playing, watching, listening, talking

- Talk about each friend and help the child to say what makes that child a friend. Think about how much the child understands about making friends.

- Listen to how they choose their friends. Are they children of the parent's friends or have they begun to make their own friendship choices?

- Reflect back what the child says, using words that describe how they feel about their friends, such as happy, excited, sad when it's time to go home.

More ideas

- Make simple plaited ribbon friendship bracelets. The child gives some to friends within the setting and saves some for new friends.

- Draw an outline of the child and use pens, photos and pictures from magazines to decorate it.

Specially for babies

- Choose three favourite rhymes or songs. Use objects as props for the rhymes if possible. Put the props and a list of the songs in a bag to take to their new setting.

- Note the ways the baby communicates with you so you can tell the new setting.

Feeling safe
Making a safe place

What you need

- A big carton
- Thin fabric
- Clothes pegs
- Soft toys
- Cushions
- Blankets

What you do

1. Tip the big carton on one side, so the child can get right into it if they wish.

2. Look together at the box, fabrics and other things you have collected.

3. Let the child climb in and out of the box, exploring it as you talk about what they are doing. Offer them a cushion, a blanket, a book or a soft toy to take into the box with them. If you can get in with them, even better!

4. Use the opportunity to explore feeling safe and not feeling safe. Ask the child where they feel safe at home, and tell them about places where you feel safe.

5. Try pegging some thin, transparent fabric (such as a net curtain or sari) to the top of the box to make a door or curtain. Explore opening and closing the door to make a secret safe place where the child is in control.

Being there – playing, watching, listening, talking

- Spend plenty of time in quiet play if that is what the child wants. Just sit and listen to the world outside, gently holding hands or with the child on your knee. When they are ready, talk softly about hiding and being safe. Listen and look for any signs of anxiety or stress.

- Singing a quiet song or lullaby will support feelings of safety and calm.

More ideas

- Add a safe light or torch to the den.
- Try a safe mirror or other reflective surface to play with.
- Listen to soft music on a CD player.

Specially for babies

- You could make a safe place for hiding games by sitting on the floor with the baby in your lap and covering both of you with a piece of light fabric or net, so you can look out at the world outside.

A bag of feelings

Finding the right words

What you need

- A picture book
- An old plain pillowcase
- Some fabric pens
- A length of ribbon
- Catalogues and magazines
- Plain paper and felt pens

What you do

1. Sit closely together and share the picture book. Take time to look at each picture and talk about how the main characters might be feeling, and how you or the child might feel in that situation. Talk about how you might know how the characters may be feeling, such as their actions or facial expressions.

2. Explain that together you could make a bag of feelings. As you make the bag together, let them talk about anything that may be worrying them.

3. Working together, decorate the pillowcase with faces with different expressions. Add the child's name and pictures of things that they have told you make them happy. Use the ribbon to tie the opening of the bag together.

4. Help the child to choose objects to go in the bag – toys that make them happy, something from the garden, pictures torn from the catalogues and magazines of things they like, and things that make them feel sad.

5. Spend time drawing pictures together of anything that is making them worried, cross or sad. Add these to the bag, tie the top and let them take it home.

Being there – playing, watching, listening, talking

- Listen for the child commenting on and reporting back their feelings and predicting ahead about what is going to happen.

- Reflect back to them what they say, and ask open questions to encourage more detail and discussion.

- Watch their body language and nonverbal communication carefully to learn more about how they are really feeling.

More ideas

- Bake some house-shaped gingerbread biscuits together.
- Make some 'feeling happy', 'feeling sad', 'feeling OK' sticky labels together.

Specially for babies

- Dance together and when the baby is smiling and happy, say 'happy baby'.
- Near the time of the move, keep any changes to routines or key workers to a minimum.

It makes me angry!

Stamping and squeezing

What you need

- Dough
- Boards
- Cutters
- Stampers
- Rolling pins

What you do

1. For many children, moving house makes them feel totally out of control, and this sometimes emerges as anger and tantrums, even in children who are usually even tempered. This activity may help with feelings of frustration and anger.

2. Sit together (either when a tantrum is just over, or at any time) and play alongside the child with some dough. Start by pummeling and squeezing the dough without using tools or cutters. The squeezing and pushing will help fingers and fists to relax. Offer cutters and tools later.

3. As the child relaxes, start to talk about feeling cross and angry. Let them know that even adults get angry sometimes. Tell them about times when you have been frustrated by things in your life (or by making up little stories about feeling out of control).

Being there – playing, watching, listening, talking

- Watch for tension in children who are facing change – tense shoulders, hands in fists, screwed up face muscles. Some children will respond to gentle massage of their hands or stroking of their shoulder. Others just find this more frustrating, so go gently.

- Monitor when tantrums or tears of frustration happen – is there a trigger at a particular time of day, an activity, an adult or other child?

More ideas

- Making bread is another great way to get rid of stress and tension.
- Try playing musical instruments, or clapping, marching and stamping to music.

Specially for babies

- Baby massage with herbal or aromatherapy oils may help to calm babies who are tense or anxious.
- Perfumed aromatherapy sprays, calming music and gentle talk also create a secure and safe atmosphere.

My moving song
Home corner big box play

What you need

- Two quoits or rings for steering wheels
- Empty boxes
- Dressing up clothes
- Small teddies and soft toys
- Blanket and tea set

What you do

1. Sing this song together in the home corner, using the words below and the tune of 'Down in the Jungle Where Nobody Goes' (This Little Puffin, E Matterson, Puffin 1991).

   Verse 1:   *Down to the new house where everybody goes*

   There's a great big lorry

   Brrm brrm it goes (pretend to steer the lorry)

   With a brrm brrrm here

   And a brrm brrrm there

   That's the way moving goes

   Verse 2:   *Down to the new house where everybody goes*

   There are lots of men with boxes, shoes and clothes
   (pile clothes in the boxes)

   With toys and books here

   And toys and books there

   That's the way moving goes.

2. Continue with other made-up verses and actions.

Being there – playing, watching, listening, talking

- Amend the verses or actions to fit suggestions from the child.

- Listen to the child as they talk about the move. Do they understand the sequence of events? Are you sure they understand that they are taking all the toys, books and furniture with them to the new home?

- Pack up the things in the home corner and move them to a new home in a tent or shelter somewhere else. You could use wheeled toys as vehicles.

More ideas

- Sing the song as you play with miniature people and a dolls' house.
- Read 'After the Storm' by Nick Butterworth about how animals feel about their new home.

Specially for babies

- Remember that singing is very important to babies. Even if you can't sing well, turn on the radio or play a CD and hum along as you rock the baby in your arms.
- Make up little songs about the baby and what they like to do.

My moving book

A personal book

What you need

- A moving story (see the resources section)
- Paper
- Stapler
- Pens and scissors
- Catalogues
- Glue-stick

What you do

1. Read one of the books about moving (see resources section), and talk about the pictures, the characters and the story.

2. Use magazines, catalogues and newspapers to find pictures of removal vans, or try the Internet (put 'removals' in Google Images) to get pictures of removal lorries. Talk about the pictures you find, and print or cut out some for a scrap book.

3. Make a simple scrapbook from paper, by folding and stapling several sheets. The cover could have a photo of the child on it, with their name and 'My Moving Book'.

4. Sit and talk while you fill the book with pictures of vans and removal men, houses, bedrooms, furniture, pets, toys and all the special things the child wants to take to their new house.

Being there – playing, watching, listening, talking

- Listen to what the child says they want to take. This will be useful when talking to parents about what really matters to their child.

- As you work together, watch the child's body language, so you can pick up tensions and anxiety when it appears, and give words of support and comfort, helping them to feel secure.

- Use a quiet, calm voice as you discuss this exciting event.

More ideas

- Use toy cars and trucks to play at removals.
- Look at some estate agents' pictures and choose a favourite house.

Specially for babies

- The coming event may not be understood by young babies, but they may well be unsettled by the packing up and disorganisation at home. Give them plenty of one-to-one support and quiet times.

My memory tree

A chance to say a special goodbye

What you need

- Small plant pot
- Pebbles to fill the pot
- A large twig with strong stem
- Thin card and felt pens
- Scissors, glue, hole punch
- Thread/narrow ribbon

What you do

1. Put the twig in the plant pot and fill with the pebbles to keep the twig upright.

2. Help the child to cut circles of card about 8cm across. Punch a hole in each card and thread ribbon through the hole so the cards can be hung on the 'memory tree'.

3. Talk together about happy times in the setting, favourite activities, special occasions and friendships.

4. Use the pens to record these memories on the card.

5. Invite the child's friends to make cards with pictures of their own to add to the memory tree.

6. Make a plant pot cover from the remaining card and ask all the children and staff in the setting to add their names before attaching it to the pot.

Being there – playing, watching, listening, talking

- Listen to the child as they describe their friendships. Acknowledge that they will miss their friends and this is sad. Talk about being busy in the new setting and how the other children will be looking forward to meeting them.

- Remind the child how good they are at making friends. Give examples of how they have joined in with activities, included other children, or played co-operatively.

More ideas

- Make a memory capsule. Decorate a cardboard tube and fill with tiny notes, pictures and photos of the child's time in the setting.

- Ask all the children to colour and put their names on a small cardboard shape. Use a hole punch and some pretty ribbon to thread the card shapes together to make a special necklace for the child leaving.

Specially for babies

- Take photos of the baby with friends at different times of the day. Make a scrap book.

- Invite the baby's parents in for a goodbye tea.

What I like, what I need

A passport

What you need

- Camera
- Mirror
- Card
- Scissors
- Glue-stick
- Felt pens

What you do

1. If possible, get hold of a passport for the child to look at, and talk about. Look at the photo and other information in the passport together.

2. Make a simple folded card passport for the child, so everyone at their new setting will know who they are and what they like.

3. If you can take a photo, talk about what the child looks like, and let them stick it on the front of the passport. If you haven't got a photo, let the child draw a picture of themselves for the front. Talk about the picture as they draw it, commenting on hair, eye colour etc.

4. Inside the passport, put pictures and words of things the child likes and things they don't like. As you make this passport together, talk about how the child can use it to help tell others about themselves.

Being there – playing, watching, listening, talking

- As you work together, you can help the child to recognise and name their likes – friends, favourite activities, food; and their dislikes. Talk about why they like or dislike things. Make sure they know it's alright to dislike some things!

- Walk round your setting if they find it difficult to choose what to put in their passport. Look at photos you have taken of the child in favourite activities and with their special friends to help their memory.

More ideas

- Put the passport in an envelope and post it together to the new setting or to the child's new address so it's there when they arrive.

Specially for babies

- Very young babies may like to watch you make their passport, listening as you talk about what you are doing.

- Older babies will love looking at a photo book all about themselves.

Advice

Some tips for practitioners:

There is much you can do to help young children cope with moving house and the upheaval and changes this often involves. You can:

- provide opportunities for the child to express their emotions

- explain what's happening in a way the child can understand

- acknowledge the child's feelings about moving

- support the child's growing emotional literacy

- help the child to find words and actions to make their feelings known

- provide an understanding and supportive environment

- find ways for the child to look positively at their changing circumstances

- be an effective listener and observer, responsive to the child's needs

- encourage empathy and understanding in other children and staff.

Tips to share with parents:

It is important for the child's key worker to discuss events with parents and talk about how their child may be responding to changes.

- Give short, simple, often repeated explanations of what is happening.

- Make sure the child understands that they haven't made the move happen – that it is an adult decision.

- Familiar things provide security – for instance, try not to get a new bed or cot at the same time as you move.

- Smells are really important to young children. Try to keep perfumes, washing powder and fabric softeners the same.

- Allow children to make some choices about where they put their things in the new house, this will help them feel at home.

- Remind children every day that all their toys and books will be taken safely to their new home.

- Not making a fuss over moving can be very powerful. Treating moving as part of everyday life will help the child to cope.

- Make time at the end of every day to talk about the day. This gives the child the chance to ask questions or have a much needed extra hug.

- Acknowledging the child's feelings is important: 'I know you feel cross about moving and I'm sorry you feel that way'.

- Talk about where everyone will be on moving day. Discuss how the child's routine can remain as familiar as possible on that day.

Resources

I want my mum!

Books

Dogger by Shirley Hughes
(Red Fox, ISBN 978 0099927907)

Alfie Gets in First by Shirley Hughes
(Red Fox, ISBN 978 009925603)

Daddy, Will You Miss Me? by Wendy McCormick
(Aladdin Books, ISBN 978 0689850639)

I Love My Mummy by Sebastien Braun
(Boxer Books, ISBN 978 1905417643)

I Love My Daddy by Sebastien Braun
(Boxer Books, ISBN 978 1905417650)

When Mummy Comes Home Tonight by Eileen Spinelli (Simon & Schuster Children's Books, ISBN 978 0689827143)

Maisy Goes to Playschool by Lucy Cousins
(Walker Books, ISBN 978 1406309713)

My First Day at Nursery School by Becky Edwards
(Bloomsbury, ISBN 978 1582349091)

Starting School by Janet Ahlberg
(Puffin Books, ISBN 978 0140507379)

I Am Too Absolutely Small for School by Lauren Child (Orchard Books, ISBN 978 1841213545)

Baby Faces by Sandra Lousada
(Campbell Books, ISBN 978 0333903986)

Captain Pike Looks After the Baby by Marjorie Newman (Macmillan, ISBN 978 1405009152)

The Little Book of Treasure Baskets
(Featherstone, ISBN 978 1904187059)

Goodnight Miffy by Dick Bruna
(Methuen Books, ISBN 978 0416194125)

Will You Come Back to Me? by Ann Trompet
(Whitman Books, ISBN 978 0807591130)

I Love You All Day Long by Francesca Rusackas
(HarperCollins, ISBN 978 0060502782).

See You Later, Mum! by Jennifer Northway
(Frances Lincoln Books, ISBN 978 1845075002).

Who Will Sing My Puff-a-Bye? by Charlotte Hudson
(Red Fox, ISBN 978 0370326665).

The Social Baby by Lynne Murray and Liz Andrews
(The Children's Project, ISBN 978 1903275016)

Websites

Take a look at Time Tracker, a highly visual, easy-to-use electronic timer from Learning Resources: www.learningresources.co.uk

For Charlie and Lola fans check out www.charlieandlola.com for simple games and lots of fun printables for making certificates.

For lots of ideas and free printable resources, visit www.sparklebox.co.uk

Visit www.communicationpassports.org.uk, www.totalcommunication.org.uk or www.ihc.org.nz for ideas and templates for communication passports that can be adapted for babies and very young children.

See www.talkingproducts.co.uk and www.inclusive.co.uk for ideas and inspiration.

It's mine!

Books

It's My Birthday by Pat Hutchins
(Greenwillow Books, ISBN 978 0688096632)

'Amazing Baby' books feature wonderfully expressive photographs of babies and a simple repetitive text. Titles include *Baby Boo!*, *Hide and Seek* and *Twinkle Twinkle*.

The Little Book of Circle Time
(Featherstone, ISBN 978 1904187943)

The Little Book of Persona Dolls
(Featherstone, ISBN 978 1904187868)

Websites

Visit http://toys.nursery-guide.info. Tiny Love is a range of pull and play activity centres, interactive baby gyms and musical mobiles.

Losing it!

Books

I Have Feelings by Jana Novotny Hunter
(Frances Lincoln Children's Books,
ISBN 978 0711217348)

The Huge Bag of Worries by Virginia Ironside
(Hodder Wayland, ISBN 978 0340903179)

I Feel Angry by Brian Moses
(Hodder Wayland, ISBN 978 0750214032)

When Sophie Gets Really Really Angry
by Mollie Bang
(Scholastic, ISBN 978 0439598453)

Rainbow Fish by Marcus Pfister
(North-South Books, ISBN 978 1558580091)

My Big Brother, Boris by Liz Pichon
(Scholastic, ISBN 978 0439968294)

Lost and Found by Oliver Jeffers
(Harper Collins, ISBN 978 0007150366)

Not Now Bernard by David McKee
(Red Fox, ISBN 978 0099240501)

But Martin by June Counsel
(Corgi Children's Books, ISBN 978 0552551380)

Owl Babies by Martin Waddell
(Walker books, ISBN 978 0744531671)

Angry Arthur by Hiawyn Oram
(Red Fox Picture Books, ISBN 978 0099196617)

Websites

Letterbox
www.letterbox.co.uk
to order a catalogue
tel: 0870 600 78 78

Kids Play Music
www.kidsplaymusic.co.uk
for musical instruments and
children's musical toys
tel: 0121 766 7561

Kids Music Education
www.kidsmusiceducation.com
tel: 07739 456 786

Speechmark
www.speechmark.net

And some resources specially for parents:

Parentline Plus
www.parentlineplus.org.uk

The NSPCC produces leaflets for supporting parents
struggling with managing their own anger and
stress as part of their 'hit means lost it' education
campaign. Find out more and download free advice
at www.nspcc.org.uk

I Can't Do It!

Books

Story and picture books to explore confidence and develop a can-do attitude:

You Can Do It, Sam by Amy Hest
(Walker Books, ISBN: 978 0763619343)

You Can Do It Too! by Karen Baicker
(Handprint Books, ISBN: 978 1593540807)

Giraffes Can't Dance by Giles Andreae
(Orchard Books, ISBN: 978 1841215655)

The Little Engine That Could by Watty Piper
(Philomel Books, ISBN: 978 0399244674)

The Owl Who Was Afraid of the Dark by Jill Tomlinson
(Egmont Books by ISBN: 978 1405210935)

Oliver Has Something to Say! (A boy who doesn't talk) by Pamela Edwards
(Lobster Press, ISBN: 978 1897073520)

When Pigs Fly by Valerie Coulman
(Lobster Press, ISBN: 978 1894222792)
I Can Do It All by Myself by Antionette Dunham
(Booksurge, ISBN: 978 1419635687)

Wibbly Pig Can Dance; Wibbly Pig Makes Pictures; *Wibbly Pig Can Make a Tent* (all great for younger children) by Mick Inkpen
(Hodder Children's Books)

Skates (Little Kippers) by Mick Inkpen
(Hodder Children's Books, ISBN: 978 0340818145)

When I Feel Scared by Cornelia Maude Spelman
(Albert Whitman & Company,
ISBN: 978 0807589007)

When I Feel Afraid by Cheri J. Meiners
(Free Spirit Publishing, ISBN: 978 1575421384)

I Can Do That! (Daisy Lane Preschool)
by Carol Matchett
(Schofield & Sims Ltd, ISBN: 978 0721711065)

I Can Do It! by Jana Novotny Hunter
(Frances Lincoln Children's Books,
ISBN: 978 1845071271)

My Day: I Can Do It by Debbie Mackinnon
(Little Brown & Co, ISBN: 978 0316648981)

When Lizzy Was Afraid of Trying New Things (Fuzzy the Sheep) by Inger Maier
(American Psychological Association,
ISBN: 978 1591471714)

The Handy Band: New Songs from Old Favourites by Sue Nicholls
(A&C Black, ISBN: 978 0713668971)

The Happy Hedgehog Band by Martin Waddell
(Candlewick Press, ISBN: 978 1564022721)

Resources

Using Stories To Help With Communication, Self-Care and Personal Skills by John Ling and Paul Chapman
(Lucky Duck Books, ISBN: 978 1412919074)

Self Esteem Games:

300 Fun Activities That Make Children Feel Good About Themselves by Barbara Sher
(John Wiley & Sons Inc, ISBN: 978 0471180272)

I Can Handle It – How to Teach Your Children Self-Confidence by Susan Jeffers and Donna Gradstein
(Jessica Kingsley Publishers, ISBN: 978 0091857479)

Helping Children to Build Self Esteem – a photocopiable activities book by Deborah M. Plummer & Alice Harper
(Jessica Kingsley Publishers, ISBN: 978 1843104889)

Websites

ParentlinePlus
www.parentlineplus.org.uk

BBC Parenting
www.bbc.co.uk
Go to: Parenting/Your Kids/Confidence Building

Who's This?

Books

Peepo by Janet and Allan Ahlberg
(Viking Children's Books, ISBN: 978 0670871766)

How are Babies Made? by Alistair Smith
(Usborne Publishing Ltd, ISBN: 978 0746025024)

Papa, Please Get the Moon for Me by Eric Carle
(Simon & Schuster Children's Books,
ISBN: 978 0689829598)

Guess How Much I Love You by Sam McBratney
(Walker books, ISBN: 978 0744549188)

Clever Daddy by Maddie Stewart
(Walker Books, ISBN: 978 0744598063)

Mama Do You Love Me? by Barbara Joose
(Chronicle Books, ISBN: 978 0811821315)

Hoot and Holler by Alan Brown
(Red Fox, ISBN: 978 0099408987)

Barfburger Baby, I Was Here First by Paula Danziger
(Picture Puffin Books, ISBN: 978 0142407394)

Baby Faces Board Book
(HarperCollins Children's Books,
ISBN: 978 0007242771)

Smile Baby Faces by Roberta Grobel Intrater
(Cartwheel Books, ISBN: 978 0590058995)

Peek a Boo Baby Faces by Roberta Grobel Intrater
(Cartwheel Books, ISBN: 978 0590058964)

This Little Baby by Sandra Lousada
(Campbell Books, ISBN: 978 0333969052)

Faces (Baby's Very First Book) (Cloth Book)
by John Fordham
(Macmillan Children's Books,
ISBN: 978 0333994177)

Websites

For lots of ideas for simple picture frames try
www.activityvillage.co.uk

ParentlinePlus
www.parentlineplus.org.uk

Net mums
www.netmums.com

Tamba
Twins and multiple birth association
www.tamba.org.uk

Where Am I Going?

Books

Story and picture books about moving:

Moving House by Anne Civardi
(Usbourne First Experiences,
ISBN: 978 0746049273)

The Berenstain Bears' Moving Day by
Stan Berenstain and Jan Berenstain
(Random House First Books,
ISBN: 978 0394848389)

We're Moving House by Heather Maisner
(Kingfisher Books, ISBN: 978 0753409978)

Goodbye House by Frank Asch
(Moonbear Books, ISBN: 978 0671679279)

Lucy's New House by Barbara Taylor Cork
(First Experiences, ISBN: 978 1577689881)

A New Home for Tiger by Joan Stimson and
Meg Rutherford
(Picture Hippo, ISBN: 978 0764101021)

Teddy Bears' Moving Day by Susanna Gretz
(Atheneum Books for Young Readers,
ISBN: 978 0689712692)

After the Storm by Nick Butterworth
(Picture Lions, ISBN: 978 0001936188)

Want That Room by Jen Green
(Hodder Wayland, ISBN: 978 0750226837)

Homer and the House Next Door by Robin Pulver
(Prentice Hall, ISBN 978 0027754575)

This Little Puffin by E Matterson
(Puffin, ISBN 978 0140340488)

Goodbye House by Robin Ballard
(William Morrow, ISBN 978 0688125264)

Websites and other resources

For removal sites, try:
www.pickfords.co.uk
www.elephantremovals.co.uk

or Google Images 'removals', 'estate agent' or 'removal van' for images, some of which you could print off.

Ask local estate agents for brochures (they may be happy to let you have the details of houses that have been sold, as they will be throwing these away).

Look at the details in the Property sections of local newspapers.

You may want to make a bag with:

• story books

• brochures

• pictures

• blank scrapbooks

• catalogues for cutting out etc.

so it's always ready to use.

Get paper doll templates from:
www.familycrafts.about.com
www.nickjr.com/parenting
www.kiddley.com
or Google 'paper dolls printable'

More resources for dealing with feelings

Talking about feelings...

The Little Book of Circle Time

Many practitioners use circle time to get children to explore their thoughts and feelings by putting them into words. This Little Book contains simple, straightforward guidance on introducing, planning and running circle time sessions.

ISBN 978-1-904187-94-3

The Little Book of Persona Dolls

Bullying, name calling, unkindness, misunderstanding are some of the issues tackled here. An experienced teacher gives ideas for using persona dolls to challenge stereotypes and help children to open their minds and understand other people and how they feel.

ISBN 978-1-904187-86-8

Dealing with Feelings

In Dealing with Feelings Jane Fisher draws on her experience as a teacher in a 'difficult' urban area. The main part of the book summarises over 100 popular children's story books (many of which are likely to already be in your setting) and shows how each can be used to encourage children to think and talk about their feelings. The included CD contains additional resources, games and templates.

ISBN 978-1-905019-56-4

Taking notice of other people...

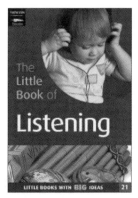

The Little Book of Listening

Why won't they listen? Here are lots of activities specially devised to encourage attentive listening, taking turns, paying attention to others and concentrating.

ISBN 978-1-904187-69-1